30-MINUTE
Frugal Vegan Recipes

30-MINUTE
Frugal Vegan Recipes

Fast, Flavorful Plant-Based Meals *on a Budget*

MELISSA COPELAND
creator of The Stingy Vegan

PAGE STREET
PUBLISHING CO.

PAGE STREET
PUBLISHING CO.

First published in 2019 by

Page Street Publishing Co.

27 Congress Street, Suite 105

Salem, MA 01970

www.pagestreetpublishing.com

Distributed by Macmillan, sales in Canada by The Canadian Manda Group.

23 22 21 20 19   1 2 3 4 5

ISBN-13: 978-1-62414-777-7

ISBN-10: 1-62414-777-1

Library of Congress Control Number: 2018964663

Cover and book design by Kylie Alexander for Page Street Publishing Co.

Photography by Melissa Copeland

Printed and bound in China

This book is dedicated to the lunch lady because no, Donna, I'm not going to just pick the meat out.

Table of Contents

Introduction

Thanks so much for picking up and taking a look through this book! You may be wondering who the heck I am, so let me introduce myself: my name is Melissa, and I'm frugal. Actually, no need to be polite, I'm more than just frugal; I'm stingy. I hate spending money and I will go to ridiculous lengths to save a couple of bucks. I was born this way.

When I was eleven years old, I decided that animal agriculture sucked. Luckily, my parents were, like, pretty cool, I guess (don't tell them I said that) and catered to my new vegetarian diet, probably thinking I'd grow out of it. Not only did I not grow out of it, but as I learned more about eggs and dairy, I decided to ditch them, too.

Now, I combine two of my most identifying character traits, stinginess and veganism, to write my food blog The Stingy Vegan (clever, eh?).

Without a doubt, the most popular recipes on my blog are the ones that can be prepared in the shortest amount of time. I get it. On a weeknight after a long day at work, no one wants to spend an hour just waiting for the tofu to press and marinate. Unfortunately, so many vegan recipes, while no doubt delicious, are ridiculously time-consuming and weirdly complicated.

On the other end of the spectrum are cheap and quick vegan recipes that are so simple that they end up being bland and boring. In this book, I wanted to write recipes for you that are not only quick to prepare but also make good use of a basic repertoire of spices, seasonings and cooking techniques to infuse maximum flavor into simple and easily accessible ingredients.

I hope you enjoy the recipes I've created for you here. While most of them are entirely new, I've also adapted a few of my absolute favorites to make them even cheaper, faster and easier. Do feel free to reach out to me via my blog with any questions or comments you may have!

A note about the recipes in this book: I am an ethical vegan (vegan for the animals first). I do not follow a whole food, oil-free, plant-based diet. Recipes include white rice, all-purpose flour and sugar because these ingredients are cheaper. You can sauté your vegetables in water or vegetable stock instead of oil, if you prefer. Whole grains can be substituted in many recipes, but the cooking time will need to be increased. Please check online for which brands of sugar are vegan-friendly (not filtered with bone char) before purchasing. And soy does not cause man-boobs.

Vegan on a Budget

If I had a cashew for every time I heard the old "I'd like to go vegan but it's just so expensive" excuse, I'd be bathing in cashew cream. There's a pervasive myth that a vegan diet is not only more expensive and complicated than the standard American diet, but that you need to do all your grocery shopping in special organic-only health food stores or from the dedicated vegetarian fridge at your local supermarket (the "but my supermarket doesn't have vegan options" excuse is another one that drives me up the wall).

It's easy to see how many people perceive veganism as expensive. Especially for those who are transitioning from the standard American diet toward a plant-based one, the fake ground meat crumbles and vegan cheeses are the easy way to eat less meat while still cooking your favorite and familiar recipes. It's true, these products are expensive, and if you base your diet around them, the costs will quickly add up.

What's not true, however, is that your supermarket doesn't have vegan options. The pillars of a healthy, hearty and delicious vegan diet are beans, rice and pasta (and maybe nutritional yeast and bananas). These are some of the cheapest items in your supermarket! They might sound boring at first, but the recipes in this book will show you how to doctor up these boring basics with seasonings, sauces and cooking methods in a way that will make you never look at a chickpea the same way again.

Let me give you some of my favorite money- and time-saving tips and tricks for eating vegan on a budget with flavorful meals that can be prepared in 30 minutes or less. Many of them may seem obvious because they are—grocery shopping and food prep is not rocket science. But if you're looking to reduce your grocery bill and save time in the kitchen, you might need to change some habits, approach shopping and cooking a bit differently and be open to trying new things.

Learn How to Really Cook with Vegetables

Yes, you can make a hearty and satisfying meal for the whole family without following the "meat and two veg" formula—you just need to have a few recipes under your belt. Follow vegan food blogs, join vegan social media groups and check out a few vegan cookbooks at your local library. Try recipes you've never tried before, try the veggie dishes at your local restaurants and, most important, keep an open mind. You think you hate tofu now? Just wait till you've tried it coated in cornstarch, panfried until crispy and bathed in a delicious sticky sauce!

Buy in Bulk

This one is a no-brainer; bulk food stores and the bulk food section of supermarkets are almost always cheaper for beans, pasta, flours and grains than prepackaged products. Also, if you've got a recipe for an unfamiliar ingredient, you can buy exactly what you need rather than risk buying an entire package that just sits in your cupboard taking up space.

Get to Know Your Local Asian and Latin American Markets

Asian markets are great for big blocks of tofu, rice, noodles, soy sauce, miso and coconut milk. Latin American markets have a great selection of beans, chile peppers, tortillas and sauces. Indian markets will blow your mind with the variety of spices offered. All of these items at better prices than supermarkets.

Don't Discriminate Against Frozen Vegetables

I know, this one can be hard. Fresh veggies taste fresh and look nice and frozen ones taste like the freezer and can cook up mushy. But science says that frozen veggies are just as nutritious as fresh, they're available year-round even when they're not in season, you don't have to worry about them rotting in a week and they're almost always cheaper. Best of all, frozen vegetables save you time. No need to wash, peel and chop them—it's already been done for you.

Grow It

I'm a big proponent of grow your own. It doesn't matter how little space you have. I live in an apartment with no balcony and I still manage to grow a small variety of vegetables. Herbs and salad greens are supereasy to grow in pots and need next to no space. Sprouts are even easier; you need no special equipment other than a jar and they are ready to eat in just a couple of days. If you've got a patio or a backyard, try your hand at tomatoes and peppers—they're guaranteed to be the most delicious you have ever tasted!

Meal Planning, Meal Prep, Batch Cooking and Freezing

All of these things boil down to one simple concept: planning ahead. Planning ahead will always save you time and help reduce food waste. Food in the garbage is just money down the drain.

First, take a look in your fridge and see what needs to be eaten before it spoils. Next, choose your recipes. You don't need to plan an elaborate menu or schedule; just have an idea of what you want to make and check which ingredients you have and which you need. (And if you're not sure you'll use up that last bit of broccoli this week or the strawberries are starting to look a little fuzzy, freeze them now.)

Then, it's grocery shopping 101: make a list and stick to it. Sticking to your list and not going grocery shopping when you're hungry will help you avoid impulse purchases and save time.

Meal prep is the next step. This involves setting aside some time to begin preparing your meals for the week. It can be something as simple as chopping a few onions and veggies, boiling some dried beans or making a pot of grains. Store them in an airtight container in the fridge to have ready to throw into your recipes throughout the week.

While planning ahead is not everyone's strong suit, cooking and freezing is a bit simpler. Have a recipe you really like? Just double the measurements, eat what you want now and freeze the leftovers for another day when you don't feel like cooking.

Use That Microwave!

Microwaves are not only for making popcorn and heating up leftover pizza; you can use them to prepare all sorts of food and in a fraction of the time it would take on the stovetop or oven.

Use your microwave to cook grains, such as rice, quinoa and barley, in half the time. Steam veggies, roast garlic, bake potatoes, make mug cakes, proof bread dough, cook pasta and do a multitude of other things you never thought possible in a microwave (seriously, just Google it!).

Avoid Packaged Foods

First and foremost, this means don't buy specialty vegan products, such as fake meats and cheeses. These are expensive.

Also avoid buying ingredients that are pre-chopped or pre-prepared. Sure, it might seem convenient to get the already-diced carrots, and maybe you think you could never get such perfect little squares, but you're literally paying someone to chop, package, brand and market that carrot for you.

Finally, learn a few simple recipes for making your own vegan staples. I like to make mayonnaise with aquafaba (the liquid from a can of chickpeas), ranch dip, sauerkraut and kimchi, confectioners' sugar and salad dressings. You can make a whole host of condiments, sauces, dressings, nut butters, plant-based milks, spice mixes and other staples with just a few simple ingredients.

Buy in Season

Produce prices at the supermarket can vary widely depending on the time of year. It's best to buy fruits and vegetables in season when they are the cheapest, the freshest and locally grown.

Pick up a seasonal food guide (and there's an app for that) or print out a list of vegetables that are in season by month and stick it up on your fridge. Plan your meals around what fruits and vegetables are the freshest and most delicious right now.

Cheap-as-Chips Main Meals

Raise your hand if you've ever had popcorn or a bowl of cereal for dinner. How many days in a row have you lived off instant ramen noodles? Am I the only one who dumps cold tomato sauce directly onto spaghetti because I'm too lazy to heat it up (and wash the pan afterward)?

I don't know anyone who wants to spend hours in the kitchen, getting dinner ready after a long day at work. That's why we grab the easiest, cheapest and oftentimes unhealthiest thing within reach. But if you can give yourself just 30 minutes in the kitchen, I'll give you a hearty main meal that's both budget-friendly and packed with flavor.

Two recipes from this chapter that have proven to be crowd favorites are the Crowd-Pleasing Mixed Bean Jambalaya (page 16) and the Spicy Thai-Style Buddha Bowl (page 36). And of course, you can never go wrong with Battered Sweet Potato Tacos (page 28) or Smoky Mushroom Fajitas (page 19). Give these wallet-friendly meals a try and save your popcorn for the movies!

Crowd-Pleasing Mixed Bean Jambalaya

This plant-based jambalaya has all the elements of its nonvegan counterpart: it's flavorful, filling and satisfying with just the right amount of spice, and seasoned deliciously. While many vegan jambalaya recipes will have you use a packaged vegan sausage product, I prefer beans, as they're not only more economical, but also heartier and healthier.

 Serves 6

1 tbsp (15 ml) oil, for pan

1 medium onion, diced

2 celery ribs, diced

½ medium red bell pepper, seeded and diced

½ medium green bell pepper, seeded and diced

4 cloves garlic, minced

1 (14-oz [400-g]) can crushed tomatoes

4 cups (945 ml) vegetable stock

1 tsp dried oregano

1 tsp dried basil

1 tsp dried thyme

1 tsp sweet paprika

2 tsp (5 g) smoked paprika

½ tsp cayenne pepper

2 bay leaves

2 tbsp (30 ml) Tabasco sauce, or to taste, plus more for serving

2 tbsp (30 ml) soy sauce

2 cups (390 g) uncooked long-grain white rice

3 cups (770 g) cooked beans (I like a mix of chickpeas, white beans and kidney beans), or 2 (15-oz [425-g]) cans, drained and rinsed

Freshly ground black pepper

1 tsp salt, or to taste

Optional garnishes: chopped fresh parsley, sliced green onion, chopped fresh cilantro

In a large saucepan, heat the oil over medium-high heat. Add the onion, celery and bell peppers and sauté until soft, 5 to 7 minutes, then add the garlic and sauté for about 30 seconds more, or until fragrant.

Add the tomatoes, stock, oregano, basil, thyme, sweet and smoked paprika, cayenne, bay leaves, Tabasco, soy sauce, rice and beans. Increase the heat to bring it to a boil, then reduce the heat to low and cover the pan. Simmer gently until the rice is cooked and the liquid is mostly absorbed, for 15 to 20 minutes, stirring occasionally, if necessary, and being sure to check that the rice on the bottom is not sticking to the pan.

Once the rice is tender, give it a taste. Add a generous grinding of black pepper and salt to taste, if necessary. Discard the bay leaves.

Sprinkle with your choice of garnishes and serve immediately with more Tabasco on the side for those who like it really spicy.

Smoky Mushroom Fajitas

Who doesn't love fajitas? Colorful sizzling vegetables and "meaty" marinated mushrooms with tons of smoky flavor all wrapped up in a handheld package. The trick here is to let them cook to the point of charring to get that extra bit of flavor. Frying the mushrooms in batches helps achieve this by giving them lots of space for their liquid to evaporate and avoid steaming.

 Makes 6 to 8 fajitas

6 to 8 (6" [15 cm]) wheat tortillas

Mushrooms

½ cup (120 ml) water

¼ cup (60 ml) fresh lime juice (from 2 limes)

¼ cup (60 ml) soy sauce

2 tbsp (30 ml) neutral oil

2 tsp (5 g) smoked paprika

2 tsp (5 g) ground cumin

1 tsp chili powder

1 tsp garlic powder

2 tsp (9 g) sugar

14 oz (400 g) oyster mushrooms, sliced into strips

2 tsp (5 g) cornstarch

Fajitas

1 tbsp (15 ml) oil, for pan

1 large onion, sliced

3 large differently colored bell peppers, seeded and sliced

½ tsp salt

Optional toppings: sliced avocado, chopped fresh cilantro, vegan sour cream or plain vegan yogurt, guacamole, salsa

If you wish, wrap the tortillas in foil and warm them in a 250°F (120°C) oven until ready to serve. Alternatively, warm them just before serving, wrapped in a towel in the microwave, for 30 seconds to 1 minute.

Then, in a large bowl, prepare the mushrooms. Combine the water, lime juice, soy sauce, oil, smoked paprika, cumin, chili powder, garlic powder and sugar. Add the sliced mushrooms and toss to coat. Leave to marinate, giving the mushrooms a stir from time to time.

To prepare the fajitas, in a wok or very large skillet, heat the oil over high heat. Add the onion and bell peppers and stir-fry until soft, 5 to 7 minutes. You can let them char in places as well; it adds more flavor. Season with the salt, transfer to a plate and cover with foil to keep warm.

Use a slotted spoon to transfer half of the mushrooms from the marinade to the skillet used for the pepper mixture, reserving the marinade. Allow the mushrooms to fry undisturbed for a few minutes on the first side until most of the water has evaporated and they are beginning to brown, then give them a stir to brown on the other side. They will reduce considerably in size. You can also let them char a bit, but be careful not to burn them. Transfer the first batch to a plate and cook the second batch.

Meanwhile, stir the cornstarch into the reserved marinade.

When the mushrooms are nice and brown, lower the heat to medium and add the first batch of mushrooms back to the pan. Give the marinade a stir and pour it into the pan. Simmer and stir for 2 to 3 minutes, or until the sauce thickens and reduces to coat the mushrooms.

Serve the warmed tortillas with the bell pepper mixture, mushrooms and any toppings of your choice.

Moroccan-Spiced Vegetables and Toasted Couscous

The fragrant mix of warming spices transforms a simple dish of vegetables and chickpeas into one that's full of flavor. Couscous must be the simplest grain in the world to cook as it only needs to be soaked, and toasting it beforehand gives it a delicious nuttiness.

  Serves 4

Vegetables

1 tbsp (15 ml) oil, for pan

½ onion, diced

4 cloves garlic, minced

1 large carrot, peeled and sliced in circles

1 medium red bell pepper, seeded and diced

1 medium zucchini, sliced into half-moons

1 tsp ground cumin

½ tsp ground cinnamon

½ tsp ground turmeric

¼ tsp cayenne pepper

1 (14-oz [400-g]) can diced tomatoes

1½ cups (360 g) cooked chickpeas, or 1 (15-oz [425-g]) can, drained and rinsed

¼ cup (35 g) raisins

1 tsp salt

Freshly ground black pepper

1½ tsp (8 ml) fresh lemon juice

Toasted Couscous

1⅓ cups (233 g) dried couscous

1⅓ cups (315 ml) vegetable stock or water

1 tsp salt, or to taste, depending on how salty your stock is

Freshly ground black pepper

3 tbsp finely chopped fresh parsley (12 g) or cilantro (8 g) (optional)

Heat a large skillet with a lid over medium heat. Heat the oil, then add the onion and sauté for 8 to 10 minutes, or until soft and transparent, then add the garlic and sauté for 30 seconds to 1 minute more, until fragrant.

Add the carrot, bell pepper and zucchini and fry for a few minutes, until they begin to soften.

Add the cumin, cinnamon, turmeric and cayenne and fry, stirring constantly, for 30 seconds, to bring out the aromas.

Add the tomatoes, chickpeas, raisins, salt and black pepper to taste. Cover the pan and reduce the heat to low. Simmer gently until the vegetables are tender, about 10 minutes.

Meanwhile, prepare the couscous. In a wide, nonstick skillet with a lid, toast the couscous over medium heat, stirring frequently so that it doesn't burn, until golden brown, 3 to 4 minutes. Turn off the heat and pour in the stock or water. Quickly cover the pan and leave to steam for 5 minutes.

Uncover the couscous and sprinkle with the salt, black pepper to taste and parsley, if using. Fluff and mix with a fork.

When the vegetables are ready, remove the pan from the heat and squeeze the lemon juice over them. Divide the couscous among 4 bowls and top with the vegetables.

One-Pan Indian-Spiced Rice Pilaf

This easy and vibrant rice dish is flavored with an exotic mix of spices and bulked up with a mix of vegetables. If you don't have all of these spices on hand and you're not sure whether you'll use them again, take a trip to the bulk food bins, where you can buy a smaller quantity. Feel free to throw in cooked chickpeas, lentils or pan-seared tofu for an additional protein component.

 Serves 4

1½ cups (293 g) uncooked long-grain white rice

2 tbsp (30 ml) oil, for pan

1 tsp cumin seeds

1 medium onion, diced

3 cloves garlic, minced

1 tbsp (6 g) minced fresh ginger

2 bay leaves

½ tsp ground turmeric

½ tsp cayenne pepper or chili powder

1 tsp garam masala (the brand I use is not spicy)

1 medium carrot, peeled and small diced

12 green beans, ends trimmed, sliced into thirds

2 cups (200 g) cauliflower florets

⅓ cup (43 g) frozen peas

3 cups (710 ml) water

1 tsp salt, or more to taste

Optional garnishes: chopped fresh cilantro, lemon or lime slices, chopped cashews, raisins, plain vegan yogurt, chutney, vegan naan or other flatbread

Put the rice in a bowl and cover with water. Gently run your fingers through the rice to remove some of the starch. Drain and repeat 2 times.

In a large saucepan, heat the oil over medium heat. Add the cumin and fry until it darkens in color and is fragrant, about a minute. Be careful not to burn it, or you'll have to start over. Add the onion and sauté for 5 to 7 minutes, or until soft and transparent.

Add the garlic, ginger and bay leaves and sauté, stirring for 30 seconds to 1 minute, or until fragrant. Add the turmeric, cayenne and garam masala and fry, stirring, for about 30 seconds, to release the aromas.

Add the carrot, green beans, cauliflower, peas, water and salt. Bring to a boil, then add the rice, cover and lower the heat to low. Cook for 12 to 15 minutes. or until the liquid has been absorbed. Remove the pan from the heat but don't uncover it. Leave it to steam for 5 minutes.

Uncover and fluff with a fork. Discard the bay leaves. Serve with any garnishes of your choice.

Easy Orange and Ginger Veggie Stir-Fry

This recipe calls for a bag of frozen vegetables. Mixed frozen vegetables are real timesavers since they're already prepped and ready for the pan. Furthermore, they help reduce food waste because you don't have to worry about them going bad. It can be tricky to cook them just right, however, as they are easily overcooked and can turn to mush. If you're not yet convinced about frozen, feel free to use your favorite combination of fresh vegetables in this stir-fry.

 Serves 4

Rice or noodles, for serving

Sauce

1 cup (235 ml) fresh orange juice (from about 2 large or 4 medium oranges)

Zest of 1 orange (about 2 tbsp)

3 tbsp (45 ml) soy sauce

2 tbsp (26 g) sugar

2 tsp (10 ml) rice or apple cider vinegar

1 tbsp (6 g) minced fresh ginger

1 tbsp (8 g) cornstarch

Stir-Fry

2 to 3 tbsp (30 to 45 ml) neutral oil, for pan, divided

8 oz (225 g) extra-firm tofu or tempeh, drained and cubed

1 (16-oz [455 g]) bag frozen mixed stir-fry vegetables (check that the veggies are not preseasoned with soy sauce or anything else. If you can't get a stir-fry mix, any mixture that looks good for a stir-fry is fine)

Salt (optional)

Optional garnishes: chopped green onion, sesame seeds, a drizzle of sesame oil, sriracha

Begin by preparing your rice or noodles according to their package directions, to serve with the stir-fry. Once you start stir-frying, it all comes together quickly.

To prepare the sauce, in a bowl, combine all the sauce ingredients and mix well. Set aside.

For the stir-fry, to keep the frozen vegetables from going soggy, I recommend using a large, wide skillet rather than a wok, to have more surface area for evaporation.

Heat the pan over medium-high heat and heat 1 tablespoon (15 ml) of the oil. Add the tofu. Fry, flipping as necessary, until it's browned and crispy on all sides, about 5 minutes. Transfer to a plate.

Add the remaining tablespoon (15 ml) of oil to the pan and let it heat up until the oil sizzles. Another trick to avoid soggy vegetables is to fry in batches so as to not steam the veggies by overcrowding. Add half of the frozen vegetables to the hot pan and fry, stirring occasionally, until hot, crisp and somewhat seared, 2 to 3 minutes. Keep in mind that frozen veggies are already parcooked, so they may cook twice as fast as fresh vegetables.

Transfer the first batch of veggies to a plate and cook the second batch, transferring them to the same plate.

Lower the heat to medium. Give your sauce a stir and pour it into the pan. Simmer, stirring, until the sauce thickens, 2 to 3 minutes. Add all of the vegetables and the tofu back to the pan and toss to coat with the sauce. Taste and add a pinch of salt, if necessary.

Serve over the rice or noodles and with any optional garnishes of your choice.

Veggie-Packed Mexican Rice

Make a big batch of this cheap Mexican rice and eat it all week. The extra veggies and beans
make it a filling vegan main dish for lunch or dinner, but you could also use it to fill
burritos or tacos or as a side to fajitas and enchiladas.

 Serves 4

1 cup (195 g) uncooked long-grain
white rice

2 tbsp (30 ml) vegetable oil

1 large tomato, roughly chopped

¼ medium onion, roughly chopped

1 clove garlic, roughly chopped

1 tsp ground cumin

1 tsp chili powder

1 tsp dried oregano

1 medium red bell pepper, seeded
and diced very small

½ small zucchini, diced very small

1 cup (150 g) canned or frozen corn

1½ cups (360 g) cooked black beans,
or 1 (15.5-oz [439 g]) can, drained
and rinsed

1 tsp salt

1 cup (235 ml) vegetable stock

1 avocado, peeled, pitted and diced

Optional garnishes: lime slices, fresh
cilantro, green onion, vegan sour
cream or plain vegan yogurt

Put the rice in a bowl and cover with water. Gently swirl your fingers through
to rinse off some of the starch. Drain and repeat 2 times. Drain very well.

In a large skillet with a lid, heat the oil over medium heat. Add the rice and toast,
stirring often, until you see golden brown spots, 5 to 10 minutes. You can leave
the rice toasting while you prep the veggies, but don't take your eyes off it for
too long, as it can quickly burn. If it's browning too quickly, turn off the heat.

Meanwhile, in a small food processor or blender, combine the tomato, onion
and garlic and liquefy. You're aiming to get 1 cup (235 ml) of puree. If you're
short, add a bit of stock, water or an extra slice of tomato to get to 1 cup
(235 ml).

Once the rice is toasted, add the cumin, chili powder, oregano, bell pepper,
zucchini, corn, black beans, salt, tomato puree and stock.

Bring to a simmer, then lower the heat to low and cover the pan. Simmer for
12 to 15 minutes, stirring once or twice to make sure the rice isn't sticking and
to check how quickly it's cooking.

Remove the pan from the heat and fluff the rice with a fork. If all of the liquid
has been absorbed but the rice is a bit underdone, leave it to stand, covered,
for another 5 minutes. Stir in the avocado and serve with any optional
garnishes.

Battered Sweet Potato Tacos

These fake fish tacos have all the essential components of a delicious Baja-style fish taco: a tangy cabbage slaw, a spicy cream sauce and crispy fried "fish," which in this case is a sweet potato!

 Makes 8 tacos

Slaw

2 cups packed (520 g) shredded cabbage

¼ red onion, thinly sliced

¼ cup (60 ml) apple cider vinegar

⅓ cup (80 ml) water

½ tsp salt

Battered Sweet Potato

1 large sweet potato (about 14 oz/400 g)

Oil, for deep-frying

½ cup (60 g) all-purpose flour

1 tsp baking powder

¾ tsp salt

1½ tbsp (11 g) taco seasoning

½ cup (120 ml) ice water (put a couple of ice cubes in a measuring cup and add water to the ½-cup [120-ml] mark)

Sriracha-Lime Mayo

½ cup (115 g) vegan mayonnaise

1 tbsp (15 ml) fresh lime juice

1½ to 2 tsp (8 to 10 ml) sriracha, to taste

¼ tsp salt

1 small clove garlic, minced

To Serve

8 small corn tortillas

Optional: fresh cilantro, sliced avocado

To prepare the slaw, pack the cabbage and onion into a 1-pint (500 ml) mason jar. Pour in the vinegar and water and add the salt. If the cabbage is not completely submerged, add a bit more water. Put on the lid and shake it up to dissolve the salt. Set aside.

Peel and slice the sweet potato into spears about 1 inch (2.5 cm) thick. Put the spears on a microwave-safe plate and microwave on high in 2-minute intervals until they can be pierced with a fork but are still firm (crisp-tender), 6 to 8 minutes. Set aside to cool.

In a deep, medium saucepan, heat the oil over medium heat. If you have a thermometer, heat to 350°F (177°C). Alternatively, you can dip a wooden chopstick into the oil, and when the oil bubbles around it, it's ready.

While the oil is heating, prepare the sriracha-lime mayo. In a bowl, combine all of the mayo ingredients.

In a separate bowl, combine the flour, baking powder, salt and taco seasoning. When your oil is hot and you're ready to fry, stir the ice water into the flour mixture to make a thick batter. Don't overmix; a few lumps are okay.

Working in batches of 3 or 4, pat the sweet potato spears dry with a paper towel. Dip each spear into the batter and then carefully drop it into the oil. Fry until golden brown, about 2 minutes. Transfer with a slotted spoon to a paper towel–lined plate.

Serve immediately on tortillas with the slaw, sriracha-lime mayo and any optional toppings.

> Note: As with anything deep-fried, you have a window of optimal crispiness before the crust starts to cool and get soggy. If you're feeding a family, you may want to start serving the tacos before you have finished frying all of the sweet potato spears. Alternatively, you can put them on a wire rack in a warm (250°F [120°C]) oven to help maintain some of their crispiness for a bit longer, but it's best to eat them right away.

Fiesta Tofu Taco Burrito Bowl with Cilantro-Lime Rice

Burritos bowls are the perfect solution for enjoying all the same flavors as a burrito but without the mess (and shame) of an improperly wrapped burrito. Burrito bowls are also great make-ahead recipes and totally adaptable to whatever veggies you have on hand or what's on sale that week.

 Makes 4 bowls

Cilantro-Lime Rice

1 cup (195 g) uncooked long-grain white rice

2 cups (475 ml) water

Zest of 1 lime

1 tsp salt

¼ cup (10 g) finely chopped fresh cilantro,

Juice of ½ lime

Burrito Bowl

8 oz (225 g) extra-firm tofu

2 tbsp (30 ml) oil, divided

½ medium onion, diced

3 cloves garlic, minced

½ red bell pepper, seeded and finely diced

¼ cup plus 2 tbsp (90 ml) tomato sauce

1 tbsp (8 g) taco seasoning

½ tsp salt, or more to taste

Freshly ground black pepper

Hot sauce (optional)

1½ cups (258 g) cooked black or pinto beans, or 1 (15-oz [425-g]) can, drained and rinsed

1 tomato, chopped

Optional additions: Diced or mashed avocado, corn, chopped lettuce, vegan sour cream, sliced lime

In a medium saucepan, combine the rice, water, lime zest and salt. Bring to a boil, then cover and reduce the heat to low so that it's very gently simmering. Simmer for about 15 minutes, or until the water is absorbed. Turn off the heat but keep the pot covered for an additional 5 minutes to steam. Fluff the rice with a fork and stir in the chopped cilantro and lime juice.

Meanwhile, prepare the other burrito bowl ingredients. Drain the tofu and squeeze it between your hands to get out some of the excess water. Put the tofu on a plate and mash it into crumbles with a fork.

In a large skillet, heat 1 tablespoon (15 ml) of the oil over medium-high heat and add the onion. Sauté for 5 to 7 minutes, or until transparent, then add the garlic and bell pepper. Sauté until the pepper is tender, about 5 minutes more. Transfer to a plate and set aside.

Add the remaining tablespoon (15 ml) of oil to the pan and increase the heat to medium-high. Add the crumbled tofu and fry, stirring, until lightly browned, 3 to 5 minutes. Reduce the heat to medium-low and stir in the tomato sauce and taco seasoning. Add the bell pepper mixture back to the pan and mix well. Add salt and black pepper to taste, and a few drops of hot sauce, if desired.

Build the bowls with the cilantro-lime rice, tofu mixture, beans, tomato and any additions of your choice.

Coconut-Lentil Curry

A bag of dried lentils will feed you for many meals. Like dried beans, they're very economical but with the added benefit that they do not need to be presoaked. That makes them great for a last-minute dinner when you don't have anything planned. This deliciously creamy lentil curry features chunks of eggplant, which help create a filling main dish, thanks to their fleshy texture. Serve this curry alone or over rice, with naan or bread on the side for sopping up the last bits out of your bowl.

 Serves 4

2 tbsp (30 ml) oil, for pan, divided

1 tbsp (6 g) cumin seeds

½ medium onion, diced

2 cloves garlic, finely diced

2 tsp (4 g) curry powder

1 cup (200 g) dried red lentils, rinsed under cold water

7 oz (200 g) frozen spinach

2 cups (475 ml) vegetable stock or water

1 (14-oz [400-g]) can crushed tomatoes

1 small eggplant, cubed

15 cherry tomatoes

1½ tsp (9 g) salt, or to taste, divided

1 (14-oz [400-ml]) can coconut milk

Cooked rice, for serving (optional)

Optional garnishes: chopped fresh cilantro, sliced lime, plain vegan yogurt, vegan naan

In a large saucepan or pot, heat 1 tablespoon (15 ml) of the oil over medium heat. Add the cumin seeds and fry for 30 seconds, or until they darken in color slightly and are fragrant. Add the onion and sauté until tender, 5 to 7 minutes, then add the garlic and sauté for 30 seconds to 1 minute more, until tender. Finally, add the curry powder and fry for 30 seconds, to release the aroma.

Add the lentils, spinach, stock and crushed tomatoes. Bring to a boil, then lower the heat to a gentle simmer and cook for 15 to 20 minutes, or until the lentils are tender but not falling apart.

Meanwhile, in a large skillet, heat the remaining tablespoon (15 ml) of oil over medium-high heat. Add the eggplant and cherry tomatoes, season with ½ teaspoon of the salt and fry until the eggplant is soft and golden brown and the tomatoes blister, about 10 minutes.

When the lentils are ready, add the eggplant mixture, coconut milk and the remaining teaspoon of salt, or to taste, to the lentils. Heat for a minute, then serve with your choice of garnishes.

No-Bake Stuffed Zucchini

This recipe is great for the abundance of cheap zucchini at the height of summer when the last thing you want to do is turn on your oven. The filling of seasoned TVP (textured vegetable protein) and mushrooms has a distinctly "meaty" texture and is full of flavor.

 Serves 2

Stuffed Zucchini

½ cup (50 g) TVP (the small crumbles)
2 medium-large zucchini
1 tbsp (15 ml) oil, for pan
½ small onion, diced
2 cloves garlic, minced
1 cup (70 g) diced button mushrooms
1½ tsp (4 g) smoked paprika
1 tsp ground cumin
2 tsp (4 g) Italian seasoning
½ tsp chili powder
¼ cup (60 ml) tomato sauce
1 tbsp (15 ml) soy sauce
Salt
Freshly ground black pepper

Crunchy Topping (optional)

1 tbsp (15 ml) olive oil, for pan
¼ cup (28 g) dried vegan breadcrumbs (I like to use panko, but regular bread crumbs work, too)
2 tbsp (16 g) nutritional yeast

Optional garnishes: vegan sour cream, plain vegan yogurt, diced avocado, your favorite chopped fresh herb, tomato sauce

Put the TVP in a bowl and cover with water. Set aside to rehydrate.

Poke holes all over the zucchini with a fork and place on a microwave-safe plate. Microwave on high in 2-minute intervals, flipping each time, until they are tender and can be easily pierced with a knife, 6 to 8 minutes. Remove from the microwave and let cool until you can handle them.

Meanwhile, in a medium skillet, heat the oil over medium-high heat. Add the onion and sauté until soft and transparent, 5 to 7 minutes, then add the garlic and sauté for 30 seconds to 1 minute, or until soft and fragrant. Add the mushrooms and leave them untouched for a couple of minutes to brown on the first side, then give them a stir to brown on the other side.

Drain the TVP. Add the paprika, cumin, Italian seasoning and chili powder to the pan and fry for 30 seconds, to bring out the aromas. Add the drained TVP, tomato sauce and soy sauce. Stir it all together and cook until heated through. Lower the heat to low.

If using the crunchy topping, in a small skillet, heat the oil over medium-high heat and add the breadcrumbs. Fry, stirring often, for a couple of minutes until golden brown. Remove from the heat and stir in the nutritional yeast.

Slice the zucchini in half and scoop out the pulp with a spoon. Roughly chop the pulp and add it to TVP mixture. Increase the heat back to medium and sauté for another minute, or until it's all well incorporated and hot.

Generously sprinkle the insides of the zucchini halves with salt and black pepper and spoon in the filling. Top with the crunchy topping, if using, and any other optional garnishes.

Spicy Thai-Style Buddha Bowl

This Buddha bowl is an explosion of textures and flavors. It starts with a simple bed of coconut rice that's piled high with a rainbow of raw veggies and crispy fried tofu. It's all tied together with a fragrant and spicy Thai red curry peanut sauce. Mango can sometimes be expensive, so feel free to replace it with canned pineapple or leave it out altogether.

 Serves 4

Buddha Bowls

1½ cups (293 g) uncooked long-grain white rice

2¼ cups (535 ml) water

1 cup (235 ml) coconut milk

1 tsp salt

1 tbsp (15 ml) oil, for pan

1 (14-oz [400-g]) block extra-firm tofu

2 tbsp (16 g) cornstarch

1 large carrot, sliced into matchsticks

¼ red cabbage (about 2 cups), shredded

20 cherry tomatoes, halved

1 small cucumber, sliced

1 small mango, pitted and diced

Optional garnishes: chopped fresh cilantro, chopped peanuts

Spicy Peanut Sauce

1 to 2 tbsp (15 to 30 ml) oil, for pan

¼ red onion, diced

1 tbsp (6 g) minced fresh ginger

2 cloves garlic, minced

2 tbsp (30 g) vegan Thai red curry paste (check ingredients)

½ to ¾ cup (120 to 175 ml) warm water, plus more if needed

½ cup (130 g) smooth natural peanut butter

3 tbsp (45 ml) soy sauce

3 tbsp (45 ml) fresh lime juice

1 tbsp (15 g) light brown sugar

Put the rice in a bowl and cover with water. Gently swirl your fingers through to rinse off some of the starch. Drain and repeat 2 times.

In a medium saucepan, bring the water to a boil. Add the rice, lower the heat to low and cover. Allow to very gently simmer—there should be just a small stream of steam escaping from the lid—for 12 to 15 minutes, or until all the liquid has been absorbed. Remove the pot from the heat but do not uncover it. Let stand for 5 minutes.

After 5 minutes, uncover the pot, fluff the rice with a fork and stir in the coconut milk and salt.

Meanwhile, prepare the sauce. In a small skillet, heat 1 tablespoon (15 ml) of the oil over medium-high heat. Add the onion and sauté until tender, 5 to 7 minutes, then add the ginger and garlic and continue to sauté for another 30 seconds to 1 minute, or until soft and fragrant. If your pan is looking dry, add up to the additional tablespoon (15 ml) of oil. Add the curry paste and fry for a couple of minutes, until the curry paste darkens in color and is very fragrant.

Transfer the curry paste mixture to a small bowl and add the remaining sauce ingredients, starting with ½ cup (120 ml) of the warm water and stirring everything together well. Add additional water as needed to reach a pourable consistency.

To fry the tofu, in a large skillet, heat 1 tablespoon (15 ml) of oil over medium-high heat. Drain the tofu and squeeze it between your hands to get out some of the excess water. Slice into cubes and put them in a large container with a lid along with the cornstarch. Close the container and shake to coat the tofu with the cornstarch. Fry, flipping as necessary, until the tofu is golden brown and crispy, about 5 minutes. Transfer to a paper towel–lined plate.

Divide the rice among 4 bowls and top with the carrot, cabbage, tomatoes, cucumber, mango, tofu and any other optional garnishes. Serve the sauce on the side.

Quick-Fix Pasta and Noodles

For good reason, pasta is a staple in most vegan pantries. It's quick, it's cheap and it's pretty hard to screw up (but not impossible). For more years than I should probably admit, I practically lived off spaghetti with tomato sauce and instant ramen; have you been there too?

I'll admit that I still practically live off pasta, but now I'm much more sophisticated (or at least I like to think so): my pasta repertoire has expanded to include not only spaghetti but all sorts of shapes, sizes and types of noodles and dishes with influences from cuisines the world over.

This chapter has its fair share of Italian-style pasta dishes, all as equally delicious as spaghetti with tomato sauce, but also includes recipes featuring rice noodles and rice vermicelli. Rice noodles are available in most large grocery stores, so if you've never cooked with them before, now's your chance to give them a try.

One thing remains the same, though; pasta is still quick, easy and a staple in my vegan pantry!

Quicker-Than-Takeout Chow Mein

This chow mein can be thrown together and on the table quicker than the delivery guy can get to your house. This recipe uses molasses to replicate the color and sweetness of restaurant chow mein without the need to buy any specialty sauces. Be sure to have all your veggies chopped before firing up the pan, as the stir-frying only takes a few minutes.

 Serves 2

6 oz (170 g) dried vegan chow mein noodles

¼ cup (60 ml) vegetable stock

2 tbsp (30 ml) soy sauce

1 tbsp (15 ml) molasses

1 tsp cornstarch

2 tbsp (30 ml) oil, for pan

2 cloves garlic, finely chopped

2 green onions, cut into matchsticks, white, light green and dark green parts separated

¼ green cabbage, shredded (about 3 cups [780 g] shredded)

2 carrots, julienned

1 cup (100 g) bean sprouts

Optional add-ins: sesame seeds, 1 tsp toasted sesame oil, salt, sriracha

Cook the noodles according to the package directions. Drain and rinse the noodles under cold water. Set aside in the colander.

In a bowl, mix together the stock, soy sauce, molasses and cornstarch to make a sauce. Set aside.

Heat a wok or large skillet over high heat and heat the oil. Stir-fry the garlic and the white and light green parts of the green onion until soft, just a few seconds, being careful not to burn them. Add the cabbage and carrots and stir-fry for a minute or two, or until the cabbage is wilted and the carrots are crisp-tender.

Add the drained noodles and stir-fry until heated through, 1 to 2 minutes.

Give the sauce a quick stir and pour it into the pan. Simmer until the sauce thickens and coats the noodles, 1 to 2 minutes. Turn off the heat and fold in the bean sprouts and dark green parts of the green onion.

Taste and adjust the seasoning, if necessary—I usually add a touch more soy sauce or salt—and add any optional add-ins you desire.

Easy American Goulash

Pasta and sauce cook in just one pot for an easy weeknight dinner that's great for chilly evenings. TVP (textured vegetable protein) is a great substitute for ground beef in this recipe and much more economical than prepackaged vegan beefless crumbles.

 Serves 4

1 tbsp (15 ml) oil, for pan

1 medium onion, diced

2 cloves garlic, minced

2 tsp (5 g) sweet (Hungarian) paprika

½ tsp smoked paprika

2 tsp (4 g) Italian seasoning

1 (14-oz [400-g]) can diced tomatoes

1 (14-oz [400-g]) can tomato sauce

2 cups (475 ml) vegetable stock

2 tbsp (30 ml) soy sauce

1 cup (100 g) TVP (the small crumbles)

1¼ cups (131 g) dried elbow macaroni

Salt

Freshly ground black pepper

Optional garnish: your favorite fresh herb

In a medium saucepan, heat the oil over medium-high heat. Add the onion and sauté until soft and transparent, 5 to 7 minutes, then add the garlic. Sauté for about 30 seconds, or until soft, then add sweet and smoked paprika and Italian seasoning. Stir for about 10 seconds to bring out the aromas.

Add the diced tomatoes with their juice, tomato sauce, stock and soy sauce. Bring to a boil, then add the TVP to the pot along with the macaroni. Lower the heat to medium-low and simmer, stirring occasionally, until the pasta is cooked al dente.

Remove from the heat and let stand for 5 minutes to thicken up. Taste and add salt if it's necessary, and pepper to taste.

Serve immediately, garnished with your favorite herb, if desired.

Fiery Chili Noodles

Just regular old spaghetti makes the base for noodles that are potent and flavorful with a healthy dose of garlic and as much sriracha as you can handle. You can use either peanut butter or tahini for the sauce, if you only have one on hand, but using the two together ensures that neither dominates.

 Serves 4

12 oz (350 g) dried spaghetti

1 tbsp (15 ml) oil, for pan

3 tbsp (30 g) finely chopped garlic (about 6 cloves)

1½ tbsp (9 g) finely chopped fresh ginger

2 green onions, chopped, white, light green and dark green parts separated

1 cup (235 ml) vegetable stock

2 tbsp (30 g) tahini

2 tbsp (32 g) peanut butter

1 to 2 tbsp (15 to 30 ml) sriracha, or to taste

1 tbsp (15 ml) soy sauce

1 (10.5-oz [300-g]) bag chopped fresh spinach

Optional garnishes: sesame seeds, chopped peanuts

Cook the spaghetti in a large pot according to the package directions. Leave some room in the pot to add the spinach at the end.

Meanwhile, in a small saucepan, heat the oil over medium heat. Add the garlic, ginger and the white and light green parts of the green onion and fry, stirring, for a couple of minutes, or until soft and fragrant.

Add the stock, tahini, peanut butter, sriracha and soy sauce and simmer, stirring often, for 3 to 4 minutes, or until thickened. Remove from the heat.

When the pasta is just about cooked, add the spinach to the pot to allow it to wilt. Drain the entire pot into a colander. Put the pasta and spinach back into the pot and toss well to combine. Add the sauce and toss to coat.

Serve immediately garnished with the reserved chopped dark green onion tops and your choice of additional garnishes.

Mint and Pea Pesto Pasta

Miso paste or nutritional yeast is the secret ingredient in this summery pesto, to give it a cheesy flavor without the Parmesan. Walnuts work great as a cheaper alternative to pine nuts. This versatile pesto is also delicious spread on toasted bread or stirred into risotto.

 Makes 2 large portions

9 oz (250 g) dried spaghetti
1 cup (130 g) frozen peas
⅔ cup (56 g) packed fresh mint
½ cup (60 g) roughly chopped walnuts, toasted
1 clove garlic, roughly chopped
1 tsp white miso paste, or 3 tbsp (24 g) nutritional yeast
Zest of 1 lemon
1½ tbsp (23 ml) fresh lemon juice
1 tsp salt
¼ cup (60 ml) olive oil
1 to 2 radishes, thinly sliced
Freshly ground black pepper

Cook the spaghetti al dente according to the package directions. Reserve ½ cup (120 ml) of the pasta cooking water before draining.

Meanwhile, bring a small pot of water to a boil and thaw the peas by simmering them for a couple of minutes. Drain and set aside about 2 tablespoons (28 g) of the simmered peas for garnish.

In a small food processor, combine the peas, mint, walnuts, garlic, miso, lemon zest and juice and salt. Blitz until you get a rough paste, then add the oil, 1 tablespoon (15 ml) at a time, and blend. It's up to you how much you want to blend it; I like to leave it with some texture.

Transfer the cooked pasta and pesto to a bowl and toss to combine. If you find your pesto a bit thick, add some of the reserved pasta cooking water by the tablespoon (15 ml) until you're happy with the consistency.

Serve garnished with the reserved peas, radishes and a sprinkling of pepper.

20-Minute Drunken Noodles

Sorry to disappoint, but there is no alcohol in these Thai-style noodles. No one knows for sure where they get their name, but the most common explanation is that they're perfect to eat after a night out drinking. Molasses replaces oyster sauce and soy sauce replaces fish sauce, for an affordable veganized version of this stir-fry. You can find rice noodles in most large supermarkets, but you'll get a better price if you have an Asian market in your area. Feel free to swap out any of the veggies for whatever you have in your fridge.

 Serves 2

6 oz (170 g) medium-width flat rice noodles

2½ tbsp (38 ml) soy sauce

1½ tsp (8 ml) molasses

2 tsp (9 g) sugar

1 to 3 tbsp (15 to 45 ml) sriracha, to taste

2 tbsp (30 ml) oil, for pan

½ red onion, sliced

3 cloves garlic, finely chopped

½ head broccoli, cut into florets

1 medium carrot, peeled and sliced in rounds

½ red bell pepper, seeded and sliced into matchsticks

15 cherry tomatoes, halved

¼ cup (10 g) roughly chopped fresh cilantro or basil, or a mix of both

1½ tsp (8 ml) fresh lime juice

Optional: A couple of lime wedges for serving, more sriracha

Bring a medium pot of water to a boil, then remove it from the heat. Soak the noodles in the hot water until al dente, 5 to 10 minutes. Drain and rinse under cold water to stop the cooking process. Set aside in a colander.

Meanwhile, combine the soy sauce, molasses, sugar and sriracha in a bowl. Place all of your prepped veggies and a glass of water next to the stove.

In a wok or large skillet, heat the oil over medium-high heat. Fry the onion until soft and translucent, 5 to 7 minutes, then add the garlic and fry for about 30 seconds, or until soft. Add the broccoli and carrot and stir-fry for a couple of minutes before adding the bell pepper. Continue to stir-fry the veggies until crisp-tender, about 5 minutes. While stir-frying, you can add a few splashes of water from time to time to help steam the veggies.

Add the tomatoes, drained noodles and sauce. Stir-fry until the sauce is absorbed, 2 to 3 minutes.

Add the cilantro and lime juice. Thai food is all about the balance of sweet, sour, spicy and salty, so feel free to add adjust the seasoning to your taste.

Serve immediately with lime wedges and sriracha on the side, if desired.

Garlicky Spring Vegetable Pasta

A cross between *aglio e olio* and pasta primavera, this recipe combines two classic recipes into one.
I like to make this when I have some random vegetable odds and ends left over from something else.
You can add whichever veggies you like; just be sure to cut them as recommended so
that they will be finished roasting at the same time.

 Serves 4 to 6

6 to 8 cups (708 to 944 g) chopped mixed spring vegetables, such as asparagus cut into 1" (2.5-cm) pieces, carrot sliced into ½" (1.25-cm) rounds, radishes quartered, broccoli and cauliflower cut into bite-sized florets, cherry tomatoes halved, and zucchini cut into ½" (1.3-cm) half moons

7 tbsp (105 ml) olive oil, divided

Salt

Freshly ground black pepper

16 oz (450 g) dried pasta of choice

4 cloves garlic, thinly sliced

½ tsp red pepper flakes

Optional: your favorite chopped fresh herb

Preheat the oven to 450°F (230°C).

Place the chopped veggies in a single layer on a rimmed baking pan. You don't want them to be crowded, so if you have a lot, it's better to divide them between two baking pans.

Drizzle with 1 tablespoon (15 ml) of the olive oil and sprinkle with ½ teaspoon of salt and a grind of black pepper. Toss with your hands to coat the veggies and put the pan in the oven (the oven doesn't need to be fully preheated to begin roasting them). If you're using one pan, place it in the center; if using two pans, place one in the upper third and the other in the lower third of the oven.

Roast until the vegetables are tender, 15 to 20 minutes. If using two pans, switch the top pan to the bottom of the oven and the bottom pan to the top of the oven halfway through.

Meanwhile, bring a pot of water to a boil and add a generous amount of salt and the pasta. Cook until just shy of al dente—1 minute less than indicated on the package directions.

While the pasta is still cooking, in a large skillet, heat 4 tablespoons (60 ml) of the olive oil over medium-low heat. Add the garlic and red pepper flakes and cook until the garlic begins to turn golden brown, 4 to 5 minutes. If the garlic is golden before the pasta is done, take the pan off the heat.

When the pasta is ready, reserve 2 cups (475 ml) of the pasta cooking water and drain the pasta. Add the reserved pasta water to the garlic mixture and increase the heat to medium-high. Simmer until reduced by half, about 5 minutes, then add the drained pasta and cook, stirring, for another minute or two, or until the pasta is al dente and is covered with the sauce.

Remove the pan from the heat and drizzle with the remaining 2 tablespoons (30 ml) of olive oil. Taste and season with salt, if necessary. Add the roasted vegetables and gently toss. Serve immediately, garnished with your favorite herb, if desired.

Creamy Artichoke and Spinach Pasta

As the price of cashews continues to rise, I've turned to coconut milk to make my creamy pasta sauces. Don't worry; the stock and nutritional yeast in this recipe ensure that the coconut flavor is not overpowering. This spinach and artichoke pasta is like your favorite dip turned into pasta. For maximum creaminess, be sure to squeeze out as much water as possible from the spinach. This super quick pasta dish is sure to become one of your favorites!

 Serves 4

10 oz (280 g) dried pasta

7 oz (200 g) frozen spinach

1 tbsp (15 ml) oil

½ medium onion, diced

2 cloves garlic, minced

2 tbsp (15 g) all-purpose flour

1 cup (235 ml) vegetable stock

Cream from 1 (14-oz [400-ml]) can full-fat coconut milk (see Tip)

1 (14-oz [400-g]) can artichoke hearts, drained and quartered

1 tsp salt

Freshly ground black pepper

1 tbsp (15 ml) fresh lemon juice

3 tbsp (24 g) nutritional yeast

Optional garnish: your favorite fresh herb

Cook the pasta according to the package directions.

Defrost the spinach. You can do this in three ways: in the microwave for 1 to 2 minutes, put it in a strainer and run it under hot water or warm it in a pot over low heat on the stove. Whichever way you thaw it, transfer it to a strainer over the sink, and when it's cool enough to handle, use your hands to squeeze out as much water as possible.

In a large skillet, heat the oil over medium heat. Add the onion and sauté until soft and transparent, 8 to 10 minutes. Add the garlic and sauté for 30 seconds to 1 minute more, or until fragrant. Sprinkle with the flour and whisk it in. Cook, stirring, for a couple of minutes to remove the raw flour taste. Add the stock and coconut cream. Bring to a simmer to melt the coconut cream, then simmer until thickened, about 3 minutes.

Add the cooked pasta, spinach and artichoke hearts. Give it a minute to heat through. Remove from the heat and add the salt, pepper to taste, lemon juice and nutritional yeast.

Serve immediately, garnished with your favorite herb, if desired.

Tip: To get the thick cream, refrigerate the can of coconut milk overnight. Open the can and scoop out the thick cream, leaving behind the water. You can keep the water if you want to use it for smoothies, but it really is just the water that the coconut has soaked in and nothing fancy.

Vegetable Singapore Noodles

This dish is all about the sauce. It's basically a curry-flavored Chinese stir-fry that's made with easy-to-find ingredients and can be modified to include whatever veggies you have on hand. I've also made it with broccoli, snow peas, baby corn and zucchini, among other things, and it's always delicious.

 Serves 4

8 oz (225 g) dried rice vermicelli

3 tbsp (45 ml) oil, for pan, divided

1 (14-oz [400-g]) block extra-firm tofu

3 to 4 tbsp (24 to 32 g) cornstarch, plus more if needed

1 cup (235 ml) vegetable stock

¼ cup (60 ml) soy sauce

1 tsp sugar

½ medium onion, sliced

2 green onions, chopped, white and green parts separated

1 large carrot, peeled and cut into matchsticks

½ large red bell pepper, seeded and sliced

2 cloves garlic, minced

1 tbsp (6 g) minced fresh ginger

1½ tbsp (9 g) mild curry powder

¾ cup (98 g) frozen peas

1 lime, cut into wedges, for serving

Optional: chopped fresh cilantro, sriracha

Bring a pot of water to a boil. Turn off the heat and add the rice vermicelli. Soak until softened, 3 to 5 minutes, or according to the package directions, then drain and rinse under cold water to stop the cooking process. You can use scissors to cut the noodles into shorter pieces, if you'd like.

In a medium skillet, heat 1 tablespoon (15 ml) of the oil over medium heat.

Drain the tofu and give it a squeeze between your hands to get the excess water out. Cut into cubes and transfer to a container with a lid. Sprinkle with the cornstarch, close the container and shake to coat the tofu with cornstarch. Add more cornstarch if you think it's necessary to get a good layer of cornstarch all over the tofu.

Fry the tofu in the heated skillet, flipping the cubes as necessary, until golden brown and crispy on all sides, about 5 minutes. Transfer to a paper towel–lined plate.

In a bowl, combine the stock, soy sauce and sugar.

In a large skillet or wok, heat the remaining 2 tablespoons (30 ml) of oil over medium-high heat. Add the onion and white parts of the green onion and stir-fry for a couple of minutes until they begin to soften. Add the carrot and bell pepper and stir-fry until softened, about 5 minutes. Add the garlic, ginger and curry powder and stir-fry for 30 seconds to 1 minute, or until fragrant and cooked through.

Lower the heat to medium and add the stock mixture, rice noodles, frozen peas and green tops of the green onions. Stir-fry for a couple of minutes, or until the noodles have absorbed the sauce.

Remove from the heat and stir in the cilantro, if using.

Divide among in four bowls and top with the crispy tofu, a wedge of lime for squeezing on top and sriracha on the side for those who like it spicy.

Roasted Red Pepper Pasta

A change from the usual tomato-based pasta sauce, this roasted red pepper sauce is thick and creamy without the need for a single cashew, thanks to emulsification. This is a great dish for peak pepper season, which is late summer and early fall.

 Serves 4

3 to 4 large red bell peppers (about 30 oz [850 g] total)

10 oz (280 g) dried pasta of choice

4 cloves garlic, unpeeled

2 tbsp (30 ml) olive oil

1½ tsp (8 ml) balsamic vinegar

1 tsp salt

Optional garnishes: several tbsp nutritional yeast, your favorite fresh herb

Bring a pot of water to a boil and turn on your broiler.

Slice the bell peppers in half from top to bottom. Remove the stem, seeds and membranes.

Place the peppers on a rimmed baking pan, skin side up. Open them up and press them down so that they are more or less flat against the pan. Place the unpeeled garlic cloves wherever there's space on the pan.

Broil for 13 to 15 minutes, or until the peppers are soft, smell delicious and the skin is black and charred in some places.

Meanwhile, cook the pasta according to the package directions.

Transfer the peppers to a large container and put on the lid. Let them steam for 5 minutes.

Carefully peel the loose skin and blackened bits off the peppers. They are still hot, so be careful not to burn your fingers. I just slide a fork under the blistered parts of the skin and peel it up. Don't worry about peeling off all the skin if some of it doesn't come off easily; it breaks down well in the blender; just peel off what is loose and black.

Squeeze the roasted garlic out of their skins. Transfer the garlic and peppers to a blender and begin blending on low speed. Once broken down, slowly drizzle in the olive oil with the blender running. Increase the speed to high and blend until smooth and creamy. Blend in the vinegar and salt.

Combine the cooked pasta with the sauce and serve sprinkled with nutritional yeast and your favorite fresh herb, if desired.

Speedy Soups and Stews

Is it a little odd that I get happy when cool weather rolls around, simply because I start thinking of all the delicious soups I can make? Soups and stews are some of my most "famous" dishes (famous in my household, I mean) and are always slurp-worthy.

With ramen, for example, you know you're obligated to slurp. When you try my Creamy Sesame Ramen (page 61), you won't be the least bit embarrassed by your noisy eating and the broth dribbling down your chin. You won't be able to think about much else other than how delicious this soup is!

The Simple Spanish Lentil Stew (page 66) and Warming Carrot-Ginger Soup (page 74) are some of the simplest recipes in this book but are great examples of how basic, cheap ingredients can be turned into something wonderful if you know how to treat them.

Do you know the trick for making vegetable stock from scraps? It's really easy and basically free. Anytime you're chopping vegetables and have some odds and ends left over, stick them in a freezer bag. Keep adding to the bag in your freezer, and when it's full, put the scraps in a pot with water and simmer for 45 minutes. Voilà, vegetable stock! You can also use all sorts of vegetable peelings and leaves; just be sure to scrub your veggies really well before peeling or choose organic.

Creamy Sesame Ramen

This is by far my favorite broth for ramen. While the majority of vegan ramen recipes rely on miso paste to make a savory broth, this one is in the style of tantanmen ramen, which makes a creamy and spicy broth from Japanese sesame paste and chili oil. Here I've used the more accessible tahini and sriracha to achieve the same basic flavor profile.

 Serves 2; can easily be doubled

2¼ cups (535 ml) vegetable stock

1 tbsp (15 ml) oil, for pan

½ (14-oz [400-g]) block firm or extra-firm smoked or plain tofu, cut into rectangles about ⅜" (1 cm) thick

Pinch of salt

8 button mushrooms, sliced

3 tbsp (45 g) tahini

2 tbsp (30 ml) soy sauce

1 tbsp (15 ml) sriracha

2 tsp (10 ml) rice vinegar or white wine vinegar

3 oz (85 g) broccoli florets

2 (3-oz [85-g]) packages uncooked ramen noodles, seasoning packet discarded

1 green onion, sliced

Optional: more sriracha to serve, sesame seeds for garnish

In a small saucepan, place the stock over low heat just to warm it up. Don't bring to a simmer—you just want to heat it, not reduce it. Also bring a medium saucepan of water to a boil.

In a medium skillet, heat the oil over medium-high heat. Add the tofu and fry until golden brown, then flip and fry on the other side until golden brown, about 5 minutes. Transfer to a plate and sprinkle with a pinch of salt.

Now, add the mushrooms in a single layer to the skillet and fry, undisturbed, until brown on the first side, about 2 minutes. Stir and fry on the other side until browned, 1 to 2 minutes more. Transfer to the plate with the tofu.

Meanwhile, in a bowl, combine the tahini, soy sauce, sriracha and vinegar. Mix well.

By now, your water should be boiling. Add the broccoli and simmer for a couple of minutes, or until tender and bright green. Use a slotted spoon to transfer the broccoli to a plate and add the ramen noodles to the pot. Simmer until tender, according to the package instructions. Drain.

Divide the tahini mixture between 2 large bowls. Ladle in the hot stock and stir to combine. Divide the noodles, tofu, mushrooms and broccoli between the bowls and sprinkle with some sliced green onion and sesame seeds, if using.

Serve with the bottle of sriracha on the side for those who like it especially spicy.

Hearty Bean and Barley Soup

Remember barley? While the recent trend for ancient grains has given quinoa and buckwheat (among others) more time in the spotlight, cheap and delicious barley has been somewhat forgotten about. Barley is particularly suited to soups and stews and the trick of parcooking the barley in the microwave while getting started on the soup reduces the total cooking time to about 30 minutes.

 Serves 4

1 cup (200 g) uncooked pearled barley

1 cup (235 ml) water

1 tbsp (15 ml) olive oil

½ medium onion, diced

2 cloves garlic, minced

1 medium carrot, peeled and diced

1 celery rib, diced

2 tsp (4 g) Italian seasoning

4 cups (945 ml) vegetable stock

1 (14-oz [400-g]) can diced tomatoes

2 cups (134 g) packed chopped kale or other leafy green

½ tsp salt, or more to taste

1½ cups (270 g) cooked white beans, or 1 (15-oz [425-g]) can, drained and rinsed

1 tbsp (15 ml) fresh lemon juice

Freshly ground black pepper

Optional: a sprinkling of nutritional yeast, more stock for a thinner soup, fresh parsley or basil for garnish, crusty vegan bread on the side

Rinse the barley in a strainer under cold water and put it in a large microwave-safe bowl or pot with a lid. For example, a CorningWare-style ceramic dish with a glass lid or a plastic microwave rice and grain cooker work well for this. If you don't have either of those, use a large nonmetal bowl covered with a plate. Just be sure that your dish or bowl is large and deep, to prevent overflow. Add the water, cover and microwave on 50 percent power for 10 minutes, or until the barley is parcooked and the water is mostly absorbed.

Meanwhile, in a large saucepan, heat the olive oil over medium heat. Add the onion, garlic, carrot and celery and cook until tender, 8 to 10 minutes, stirring frequently and being careful not to burn the onion and garlic.

Add the Italian seasoning and stir for about 30 seconds to release the flavors. Add the stock, tomatoes with their juice, parcooked barley, kale (if you're using a more tender green, such as spinach, wait to add it at the end) and the salt. Cover the pot and increase the heat to bring to a boil, then lower the heat and simmer gently partially covered. Simmer for 15 minutes, or until the barley and kale are tender.

Add the beans and give them a minute to heat through before removing the pot from the heat. Stir in the lemon juice. Taste and add more salt, if necessary (depends on how salty your stock is), and pepper to taste.

Serve immediately with your choice of garnishes and crusty vegan bread.

Note that the soup will thicken as it sits, so if you have leftovers, you may need to add a few more splashes of stock or water when reheating.

Flavorful African Peanut Stew

If you've never tried African peanut stew before, a glance over the ingredients listed here might leave you skeptical. Peanut butter, cumin and tomatoes? What is this crazy stew? But one taste and you'll be hooked, I promise. This dish can be served anywhere from a thick stew to a soup. This recipe is on the thicker side, but you can thin the consistency with a bit more stock, if you prefer. Because this stew freezes great, it's worth it to make a large batch to keep on hand for those days that you need dinner super fast.

 Serves 4

1 tbsp (15 ml) oil

1 medium onion, diced

1 tbsp (6 g) minced fresh ginger

4 cloves garlic, minced

1 medium sweet potato, peeled and cut into 1" (2.5-cm) dice

2 tsp (5 g) ground cumin

½ tsp cayenne pepper

2 cups (475 ml) vegetable stock

1 (14-oz [400-g]) can diced tomatoes

½ cup (130 g) smooth natural peanut butter

1 tsp salt

2 cups packed (72 g) chopped Swiss chard or spinach

1½ cups (360 g) cooked chickpeas, or 1 (15-oz [425-g]) can, drained and rinsed

Freshly ground black pepper

Cooked rice, millet or quinoa, for serving

Optional garnishes: fresh cilantro, chopped peanuts

Bring a pot of water to a boil to cook the grain you will serve with the stew.

In a separate large pot, heat the oil over medium-high heat. Add the onion, ginger and garlic and sauté until the onion is soft and transparent, 5 to 7 minutes. Add the sweet potato and sauté for about 3 minutes, until it begins to soften.

Add the cumin and cayenne and sauté, stirring, for 30 seconds to 1 minute, to bring out the flavors. Add the stock, tomatoes with their juices, peanut butter and salt. Cover and bring to a boil, then lower the heat to a simmer.

Simmer for 10 to 15 minutes, stirring occasionally, until the sweet potato is tender.

Add the Swiss chard, chickpeas and black pepper. You can be generous with the black pepper in this stew! Give the stew a couple more minutes on the stove, to wilt the chard and heat the chickpeas through. You can thin the stew with more veggie stock or water, if desired.

Serve the stew over your favorite grain, cooked according to its package directions, and garnished with cilantro and peanuts, if desired.

Simple Spanish Lentil Stew

This simple and economical lentil stew doesn't look like much on paper but comes together into a comforting and warming plant-based dish that's equally good for a chilly winter evening as it is for a barbecue or potluck side dish. You can use lentils that you've previously cooked during your weekly meal preparations or canned lentils.

 Serves 4

1 tbsp (15 ml) oil, for pan

1 medium onion, finely diced

2 cloves garlic, minced

1 medium green bell pepper, seeded and finely diced

1 large tomato, finely diced

1½ tsp (4 g) smoked paprika

2 cups (475 ml) vegetable stock

2 cups (475 ml) water

2 medium carrots, finely diced

1 large potato, peeled and finely diced

3 cups (594 g) cooked lentils, or 2 (15-oz [425-g]) cans, drained and rinsed

2 tbsp (30 ml) soy sauce

1 tsp salt

Freshly ground black pepper

Optional garnishes: your favorite fresh herb or chopped green onion

In a medium saucepan, heat the oil over medium heat. Add the onion, garlic, bell pepper and tomato and cook until everything is very soft, 10 to 15 minutes. You want these to meld into the stew rather than be crisp, so take your time and let them get really soft.

Add the smoked paprika and fry, stirring continuously, for 30 seconds, to bring out the aroma.

Add the stock, water, carrots and potato. Bring to a boil, then lower the heat to a simmer and cook until the carrots and potatoes are soft, 7 to 10 minutes.

Stir in the lentils, soy sauce, salt and black pepper and give it another couple of minutes to heat the lentils through.

Thicken the stew either with a couple blitzes of an immersion blender or by transferring a couple of ladlefuls to a blender and then pouring back into the pot.

Serve with any of the optional garnishes.

Cuban-Style Black Bean Soup

Whereas Cuban black beans are normally long simmered and made from scratch with dried beans, we can cut some corners here by using canned beans with their aquafaba (the liquid in the can) and a quick blitz with an immersion blender to thicken.

 Serves 2 as a main, 4 as a starter

2 tbsp (30 ml) oil, for pan

½ medium onion, diced

½ medium green bell pepper, seeded and diced

2 cloves garlic, minced

1 tsp dried oregano

1 tsp ground cumin

2 (15.5-oz [439-g]) cans black beans, undrained

1 cup (235 ml) water

1½ tsp (8 ml) red or white wine vinegar

1½ tsp (6 g) sugar

Salt, to taste

Optional garnishes: chopped avocado, cilantro, green onion, vegan sour cream or plain vegan yogurt

In a medium saucepan, heat the oil over medium-low heat and fry the onion, bell pepper and garlic until soft, 10 to 15 minutes. Add the oregano and cumin and fry, stirring, for 30 seconds, to release their aromas.

Pour in the entire contents of the cans of beans and the water. Increase the heat to bring to a gentle simmer and simmer for 5 minutes to soften the beans a bit.

Turn off the heat and add the vinegar and sugar. Taste and add salt, if necessary (depends on how salty your beans were).

Puree some of the soup to thicken it, still leaving lots of beans. You can do this either with an immersion blender or by ladling some of the soup into a blender and then returning it to the pot. I like to puree about a third to half of the soup.

Serve plain or with your choice of garnishes.

Hot and Sour Soup

This Chinese restaurant classic is surprisingly quick and easy to make at home and equally satisfying as the restaurant version. This is the soup that gets us excited for soup season every year! Shiitake mushrooms, bamboo shoots, tofu and rice vinegar are all available in large supermarkets, but a trip to an Asian market, if you have one nearby, will get you a better deal.

 Serves 4

6 cups (1.4 L) vegetable stock

2 cups (134 g) sliced shiitake mushrooms (about 4 large)

1 (8-oz [227-g]) can sliced bamboo shoots, drained

8 oz (227 g) extra-firm tofu, cubed

1 large carrot, peeled and cut into matchsticks

1 tbsp (6 g) minced fresh ginger

2 cloves garlic, minced

¼ cup (60 ml) soy sauce

¼ cup (60 ml) rice vinegar, or more to taste

3 tbsp (24 g) cornstarch

¼ cup (60 ml) water

Freshly ground black pepper

Salt

1 green onion, chopped

In a large saucepan, bring the stock to a boil. Add the mushrooms, bamboo shoots, tofu, carrot, ginger, garlic, soy sauce and vinegar. Bring back to a boil, then lower the heat to a simmer and allow to simmer for 10 minutes, or until the carrot is tender.

In a small bowl, dissolve the cornstarch in the water. Add it to the soup and simmer for a couple more minutes, for the soup to thicken.

Add a generous grinding of pepper. Taste and add salt, if necessary (I usually add 1 teaspoon, but it depends how salty your stock is) and you can add more vinegar if you like it especially sour (I usually add 1 more tablespoon [15 ml]).

Serve garnished with green onion.

Lasagna Soup

Lasagna soup is a super easy, no-fuss recipe that's wonderfully hearty and comforting. Since older lentils can take longer to cook, starting them off in a separate pot ensures that they are perfectly tender by the time the rest of the soup is ready.

 Serves 6

¾ cup (150 g) dried brown lentils

1 tbsp (15 ml) oil, for pan

½ medium onion, diced

½ small zucchini, diced small

1 medium carrot, peeled and diced small

2 cloves garlic, minced

2 tbsp (32 g) tomato paste

2 tsp (4 g) Italian seasoning

1 (14-oz [400-g]) can diced tomatoes

1 (14-oz [400-g]) can crushed tomatoes

4 cups (925 ml) vegetable stock

8 oz (225 g) dried mafalda pasta or lasagna noodles, broken into 2" (5-cm) pieces

1 tsp salt, or to taste

Freshly ground black pepper

Optional garnishes: your favorite chopped fresh herb, a dollop of vegan sour cream or cashew or tofu ricotta, vegan Parmesan

Bring a small saucepan of water to a boil. Rinse the lentils under running water and pick out any stones. Drain and add to the water when it boils. Simmer until tender. The cooking time can vary depending on how fresh your lentils are, so start checking after 15 minutes. Drain when ready.

In a large saucepan, heat the oil over medium-high heat. Add the onion and sauté until soft and transparent, 5 to 7 minutes, then add the zucchini and carrot. Fry for a couple of minutes, until crisp-tender. Add the garlic and sauté, stirring, for about 30 seconds, or until fragrant. Add the tomato paste and Italian seasoning and fry, stirring, for another 30 seconds.

Add the diced tomatoes and their juice, crushed tomatoes and their juice and stock. Cover the pot and increase the heat to bring to a boil. Remove the lid, add the pasta and lower the heat to a simmer.

Simmer for the length of time indicated on the package of pasta (mine says 9 minutes until al dente). Remove from the heat and add the drained cooked lentils, salt and pepper to taste (it depends on how salty your stock is). If you'd like a thinner soup, feel free to add water or a bit more stock.

The soup is best served immediately, as the pasta will continue to absorb the liquid as it sits. Serve plain or with your choice of garnishes.

If you have leftovers for the next day, reheat the soup in a pot with a few splashes of water or stock to thin it out a bit.

Warming Carrot-Ginger Soup

This recipe is so simple yet so delicious. I tried many, many variations on this recipe—and it almost didn't make it into the book—before realizing that most delicious way to make this soup was by roasting the carrots to bring out their natural sweetness. It's now one of my favorite soups!

 Serves 6

2 lb (900 g) carrots (about 8 large)

2 tbsp (30 ml) olive oil, divided

Sprinkling of salt

Pinch of freshly ground black pepper

1 large onion, diced

2 cloves garlic, finely chopped

1 tbsp (6 g) finely chopped fresh ginger

4 cups (945 ml) vegetable stock, plus more (or water) to taste

Optional garnishes: a drizzle of coconut milk, vegan croutons, microgreens, pumpkin seeds, your favorite fresh herb, etc.

Preheat the oven to 450°F (230°C).

Peel and slice the carrots into rounds no more than ½ inch (1.3 cm) thick. Place them on a baking pan, drizzle with 1 tablespoon (15 ml) of the olive oil and sprinkle with salt and pepper. Toss to coat and put the pan in the oven (the oven can still be preheating). Roast, stirring and tossing a couple of times, until tender and beginning to brown, 15 to 20 minutes.

Meanwhile, in a medium saucepan, heat the remaining tablespoon (15 ml) of oil over medium-low heat. Add the onion and a pinch of salt. Fry gently until soft, 10 to 15 minutes, then add the ginger and garlic and continue to fry for a couple more minutes, or until soft and fragrant. No need to rush this step since you're waiting for the carrots and the lower heat will bring out more flavors.

When the carrots are just about done, add the stock to the saucepan, increase the heat and bring to a boil. Blend the carrots into the soup: If you're using a blender, combine the carrots and the contents of the pot (careful, it's hot—you may need to do this in batches) in the blender, being careful to allow the steam to escape. If you're using an immersion blender, add the carrots directly to the pot and blend.

This makes a thick soup; you can add more stock or water to thin it out, if you like (I add an additional ½ cup [120 ml]). Taste and season with salt and pepper, if necessary (depends how salty your stock is) and your choice of optional garnishes.

Red Curry Noodle Soup

In less than 30 minutes, you can have a soup that tastes as if it's been simmering all day. The secret is the Thai red curry paste, which brings all the flavor to the party with no work on your part, and can be found in most supermarkets. This delicious broth combined with a mixture of vegetables— feel free to use whatever is in season—and rice noodles make for one slurp-worthy soup.

 Serves 4

6 oz (175 g) dried rice vermicelli

2 tbsp (30 ml) oil, for pan

3 tbsp (45 g) vegan Thai red curry paste (check ingredients)

3 cups (710 ml) vegetable stock

1 (14-oz [400-g]) can coconut milk

½ head broccoli, cut into florets

12 green beans, ends trimmed, sliced into 3 pieces

2 medium carrots, peeled and sliced

1 tbsp (15 ml) soy sauce

1 tsp sugar

1 tbsp (15 ml) fresh lime juice

16 cherry tomatoes, quartered

Optional garnishes: ½ cup (20 g) chopped fresh cilantro, ¼ cup (35 g) roughly chopped peanuts, lime wedges

Bring a pot of water to a boil, then turn off the heat. Add the rice vermicelli and soak until soft, 3 to 5 minutes. Drain in a colander and rinse with cold water to stop the cooking process.

In a saucepan, heat the oil over medium heat. Add the curry paste and fry, stirring frequently, until it has darkened in color and is very fragrant, about 5 minutes. If it starts to stick on the bottom of the pot, add a few splashes of vegetable stock.

Add the stock, coconut milk, broccoli, green beans and carrots. Increase the heat to bring to a boil, then lower to a gentle simmer. Simmer until the veggies are crisp-tender, 5 to 10 minutes.

Add the soy sauce, sugar and lime juice. Taste and adjust the seasonings as necessary. Remove from the heat.

Divide the noodles among 4 bowls and ladle the soup over them. Garnish each bowl with cherry tomatoes and your choice of garnishes.

Plant-Powered Salads

A salad in my house is never pathetic. No limp lettuce and watery tomato here. Salads need to be real food, so packed with veggies, grains, beans or noodles that they put snoozefest iceberg lettuce–tomato-cucumber salads to shame.

Salads are a great way to showcase seasonal produce. The Autumn Harvest Barley Salad (page 80) features the best way to enjoy winter squash: roasting. Roasted squash is so sweet and delicious that it's almost like candy. The Chili-Lime Melon Salad (page 88) makes the best of the summer's melons, which are also some of the cheapest fruit per pound you can buy.

Many of the salads in this chapter are hearty enough stand alone as a whole meal or they can be served as a side along with a sandwich, soup or stew. The Eat the Rainbow Avocado Pasta Salad (page 87) and Classic Three-Bean Salad (page 95) are great contributions to a barbecue, picnic or potluck.

So, forget what you think about salads being plain and boring, and fill up your plate with one of these satisfying and delicious plant-powered salads.

Autumn Harvest Barley Salad

Autumn just might be my favorite season, as there's nothing more delicious and versatile than a winter squash. Filled with hearty barley and squash, roasted to enhance its sweetness, this autumn harvest salad is abundant and filling enough for a stand-alone main meal or as a side dish for a special occasion.

 Serves 4

Salad

½ cup (100 g) uncooked pearled barley

1 cup (235 ml) water or vegetable stock

Salt

Freshly ground black pepper

1 small squash (I use red kuri that weigh about 1.5 lb [680 g]. Any kind of squash or even sweet potato will work.)

Drizzle of oil

8 cups (440 g) mixed salad greens

1 apple, cored and sliced or diced

¼ cup (30 g) dried cranberries

2 tbsp (18 g) pumpkin seeds

Dressing

2 to 6 tbsp (30 to 90 ml) water, or as necessary

¼ cup (60 g) tahini

2 tbsp (30 ml) brown rice syrup, pure maple syrup, or agave nectar

2 tbsp (30 ml) fresh lemon juice

½ tsp salt

1 small clove garlic, minced (omit if you don't like raw garlic)

Preheat the oven to 400°F (200°C).

In a strainer, rinse the barley under cold water. In a microwave-safe dish with a lid, combine the barley and water or stock. For example, a CorningWare-style ceramic dish with a glass lid or a plastic microwave rice and grain cooker work well for this. If you don't have either of those, use a large nonmetal bowl covered with a plate. Just be sure that your bowl is large and deep, to prevent overflow. Cover and microwave on 50 percent power for 20 minutes. If it's your first time cooking barley in the microwave, keep an eye on it, since every microwave oven cooks differently and you don't want to over- or undercook it. It's done when it's tender and all the water has been absorbed. Fluff with a fork and season with salt and pepper.

Meanwhile, carefully cut your squash in half and scoop out the seeds (reserve the seeds to roast another time). Slice into 1-inch (2.5-cm) slices and place on a baking sheet. Drizzle with a touch of oil and a pinch of salt and pepper. Toss to coat each piece and arrange in a single layer on the pan. Roast until tender, 15 to 20 minutes (you can start roasting even while the oven is still preheating).

To prepare the dressing, in a small bowl, stir together all the dressing ingredients, starting with 2 tablespoons (30 ml) of water and adding more as needed to reach a pourable consistency. You can adjust the flavors if you'd like more sweetener or lemon.

In a large bowl, gently toss together the salad greens, barley, apple slices, squash slices, dried cranberries and pumpkin seeds.

Serve with the dressing on the side to drizzle over the salad.

Vietnamese Tofu Noodle Salad

This light and refreshing rice vermicelli salad features crisp raw vegetables, flavorful fried tofu and a tangy dressing. This noodle dish makes a great summertime lunch or light dinner. Keeping a few pots of herbs on your windowsill or in your garden for throwing into recipes like this one is not only easy to do, but will also save you tons of money over the course of a year.

 Serves 2

Salad

4.5 oz (125 g) rice vermicelli

1 small carrot, julienned

½ medium cucumber, sliced

2 radishes, sliced

½ cup (20 g) fresh cilantro, mint or basil (preferably a combination of at least 2)

¼ cup (35 g) peanuts, roughly chopped

2 green onions, sliced

Dressing

¼ cup (60 ml) fresh lime juice

2 tbsp (30 ml) soy sauce

2½ tsp (11 g) sugar

1 to 2 tsp (5 to 10 ml) sriracha

½ clove garlic, minced

Tofu

7 oz (200 g) extra-firm tofu, drained

1 to 2 tbsp (8 to 16 g) cornstarch

2 tbsp (30 ml) oil, for pan

2 tbsp (30 ml) soy sauce

2 tsp (9 g) sugar

1 to 2 tsp (5 to 10 ml) sriracha

Bring a pot of water to a boil, then turn off the heat. Add the rice vermicelli and soak until soft, 3 to 5 minutes. Drain in a colander and rinse with cold water to stop the cooking process.

To prepare the dressing, in a small bowl, combine all of the dressing ingredients and set aside.

Slice the tofu into rectangles or cubes about ½ inch (1.3 cm) thick. Place the tofu slices and cornstarch in a plastic bag or container, seal, and shake to coat the tofu with the cornstarch. Add more cornstarch as necessary so that the tofu is well coated.

In a medium skillet, heat the oil over medium-high heat. Add the tofu slices and fry, flipping once, until golden brown on both sides, about 5 minutes.

Meanwhile, in a small bowl, combine the soy sauce, sugar and sriracha. Once the tofu is fried, pour the sauce into the pan. Stand back as you do so, as the oil may splatter. Allow the sauce to reduce and flip the tofu once so that it is coated in a sticky sauce on both sides.

Toss the cooked noodles with half of the dressing. If the noodles have stuck together, just give them a quick rinse with cold water and drain again. Divide the noodles between 2 bowls and top with the tofu and the carrot, cucumber, radishes, cilantro, peanuts and green onions. Serve the remaining dressing on the side, to spoon on as you eat.

Spinach, Orange and Date Couscous Salad

Sweet dates, nutty toasted couscous, juicy oranges and a fruity dressing make this a complex and interesting spinach salad with Middle Eastern influences. While Medjool dates are all the rage in vegan cooking, they are much too expensive for me. I use smaller regular dates and they are a good item to buy from the bulk bins.

 Serves 2 as a main, 4 as a side

Couscous

1 cup (175 g) uncooked couscous

1 cup (235 ml) water

½ tsp salt

Freshly ground black pepper

Dressing

Zest and juice of 1 large orange (about ¼ cup [60 ml] juice) plus reserved juice squeezed from the membranes of the segmented oranges

2 tbsp (30 ml) olive oil

1 tbsp (15 ml) apple cider vinegar

¼ tsp salt

2 tsp (10 ml) agave nectar, brown rice syrup or pure maple syrup

Salad

2 large oranges, segmented (see Note; squeeze and reserve the juice from the membranes for the dressing)

2 cups (60 g) chopped or baby spinach

¼ red onion, finely diced

3 tbsp (18 g) thinly sliced fresh mint

¼ cup (36 g) toasted sunflower or pumpkin seeds

6 oz (175 g) dates, pitted and roughly chopped

To prepare the couscous, in a dry skillet with a lid, toast the couscous over medium heat until golden brown, 3 to 4 minutes. Remove the pan from the heat, pour in the water and cover. Set aside for 5 minutes. Uncover, sprinkle in the salt and pepper and fluff with a fork.

For the dressing, in a bowl, combine all of the dressing ingredients.

Mix together the couscous with the orange slices, spinach, red onion, mint, sunflower seeds and dates. Add the dressing and toss to combine.

Serve immediately.

> Note: To segment an orange, slice off the top and bottom. Stand it on one end and slice off the skin, using downward strokes from top to bottom. Slice between the membranes to segment the orange into slices.

Eat the Rainbow Avocado Pasta Salad

This avocado pasta salad is a fifteen-minute recipe that can be prepped ahead and is great to take along to a picnic, barbecue, potluck or as an easy weeknight dinner. This no-mayo pasta salad is deliciously creamy and packed full of fresh veggies.

 Serves 6

Salad

8 oz (225 g) dried salad pasta of your choice

3 cups (360 g) cooked chickpeas, or 2 (15-oz [425-g]) cans, drained and rinsed

1 cucumber, chopped

½ medium red bell pepper, seeded and diced

½ medium red onion, thinly sliced

2 celery ribs, chopped

8 oz (225 g) cherry tomatoes, quartered

Avocado Dressing

1 avocado, peeled, pitted and roughly chopped

¾ cup (175 ml) water

1 clove garlic

2 tbsp (30 g) horseradish or Dijon mustard

1½ tsp (2 g) dried dill

1 tsp salt

Freshly ground black pepper

Cook the pasta according to the package directions. Drain and set aside to cool.

To prepare the dressing, in a blender or food processor, combine the avocado, water, garlic, horseradish, dill, and salt and black pepper to taste.

Toss the cooled pasta with the chickpeas, cucumber, bell pepper, red onion, celery, tomatoes and the avocado dressing. Taste and adjust the seasonings, if necessary.

Serve immediately or refrigerate until ready to serve. The assembled salad keeps for a couple of days in the fridge.

Chili-Lime Melon Salad

When melons are in season, they are some of the cheapest fruits available, so be sure to take advantage during the summer months. The dressing for this salad is sweet, tart and fresh with just a hint of spice to liven things up.

 Serves 4 as a side

Salad

4½ cups (720 g) diced melon, preferably a mix of watermelon, honeydew and cantaloupe (½"[1.25-cm dice])

½ small cucumber, thinly sliced

2 tbsp (20 g) very finely diced red onion

4 radishes, thinly sliced

20 fresh mint leaves, roughly chopped (about 3 tbsp [18 g])

2 tbsp (18 g) chopped peanuts

Dressing

1 tbsp (15 ml) fresh lime juice

2 tsp (10 ml) soy sauce

1 tsp light brown sugar

½ tsp sriracha

½ tsp grated fresh ginger

Place the melon cubes in a colander to drain some of their water while you prepare the remaining ingredients.

To prepare the dressing, in a small bowl or mason jar, combine the lime juice, soy sauce, brown sugar, sriracha and ginger. Stir or shake to dissolve the sugar.

In a large bowl, toss together the cucumber, red onion, radishes and melon cubes. Arrange the salad on a serving dish, drizzle with the dressing and garnish with the mint and peanuts.

Serve immediately.

Curry-Roasted Vegetable Salad

This salad uses super cheap produce but certainly does not lack in the flavor department. Roasting brings out the sweetness of the vegetables, while a light dusting of curry powder adds a punch of flavor. The lentils add a nutritional boost and help fill you up.

 Serves 4

Salad

½ cup (100 g) dried lentils, or about 1½ cups (297 g) cooked (a small variety, such as black caviar or Puy, is nice, but regular brown will work, too)

½ medium cauliflower, cut into florets

4 medium carrots, peeled and sliced into ½" (1.25-cm) coins

2 tbsp (30 ml) olive oil, divided

1 tsp curry powder

¾ tsp salt, divided

Freshly ground black pepper

6 cups (402 g) chopped kale or other leafy green

Hummus Dressing

⅓ cup (82 g) hummus

1 tbsp (15 ml) fresh lemon juice

1 small or ½ medium clove garlic, minced

1½ (8 ml) tsp pure maple syrup, brown rice syrup or agave nectar

¼ tsp salt

1 tbsp (15 ml) or more water, to thin

½ tsp curry powder

Preheat the oven to 450°F (230°C).

Bring a small pot of water to a boil. Rinse the lentils under running water and pick out any stones. Drain and add to the water when it boils. Simmer over medium-low heat until tender, 20 to 30 minutes, depending on the size and freshness of the lentils.

Meanwhile, arrange the cauliflower florets and carrots on a baking sheet. Drizzle with 1½ tablespoons (23 ml) of the oil and sprinkle with the curry powder, ½ teaspoon of the salt and pepper. Get in there with your hands and toss it up to coat the veggies all over.

Put the pan in the oven (the oven does not have to be fully preheated) and roast the veggies for 15 to 20 minutes, tossing halfway through, or until tender and beginning to brown.

Meanwhile, if you're using kale, you may want to give it a little massage. Put the kale in a large bowl and drizzle with 1½ teaspoons (8 ml) of the olive oil and the remaining ¼ teaspoon of salt. Massage for a couple of minutes to tenderize.

To prepare the dressing, in a small bowl, combine all of the dressing ingredients. If you're using store-bought hummus, the flavor can vary a lot from brand to brand; some are more sour, others more garlicky. I recommend tasting the hummus before deciding how much lemon juice, garlic, maple syrup and salt to add. Add enough water to reach a pourable consistency. You can add more curry powder if you want a more pronounced curry flavor.

Once the veggies are roasted and the lentils are tender, toss them together with the greens. Serve with the dressing.

Summery Peach and Tomato Panzanella

Panzanella is a simple, rustic Italian bread-and-tomato salad that bursts with flavor despite its humble ingredients. This recipe goes beyond the classic by adding peaches for an extra pop of summery sweetness.

 Serves 4

Salad

15 oz (425 g) cherry tomatoes, sliced in half

2 large peaches, sliced and pitted

1 tsp salt, plus more to taste

½ loaf vegan ciabatta bread

½ small red onion, finely diced

¼ cup packed (10 g) fresh basil, roughly chopped

Freshly ground black pepper

Vinaigrette

¼ cup (60 ml) olive oil

2 tbsp (30 ml) red or white wine vinegar

1 small clove garlic, minced

Place the halved tomatoes and peaches in a colander set over a bowl to collect the juices. Sprinkle with 1 teaspoon of salt and stir. Set aside for 20 minutes while you prepare the rest of the salad, stirring from time to time to release more juice.

Preheat the broiler.

Slice or tear the bread into pieces more or less the same size as your halved tomatoes. Place in a single layer on a baking sheet and broil until toasted, tossing once. It only takes a couple of minutes, so don't walk away, as they will burn quickly.

To prepare the vinaigrette, in a bowl or mason jar, stir or shake together the olive oil, vinegar and garlic.

When you're ready to serve, add the tomato and peach juice to the vinaigrette and mix well. Assemble the salad: In a large bowl, combine the tomatoes, peaches, red onion, basil and toasted bread. Add the vinaigrette, toss well and season to taste with salt and pepper.

Classic Three-Bean Salad

Three-bean salad is a perfect make-ahead dish. It takes just ten minutes to prepare and can be refrigerated until ready to serve. It actually gets better the longer you leave it, as the beans soak up the yummy sweet and sour dressing. It's great bring along to a barbecue or potluck.

 Serves 6

10 oz (283 g) fresh green beans

1½ cups (360 g) cooked chickpeas, or 1 (15-oz [425-g]) can, drained and rinsed

1½ cups (360 g) cooked kidney beans, or 1 (15-oz [425-g]) can, drained and rinsed

2 celery ribs, chopped

¼ cup (15 g) chopped fresh parsley

Dressing

⅓ cup (80 ml) apple cider vinegar

3 tbsp (45 ml) olive oil

¼ cup (50 g) sugar

1 tsp salt

Freshly ground black pepper

Trim the ends off the green beans, then slice them into thirds. Place in a microwave-safe bowl and add enough water to cover the bottom of the bowl. Cover the bowl with a lid or a plate and microwave on high for 4 to 6 minutes, or until the beans are tender. Drain and let cool for a few minutes.

Meanwhile, prepare the dressing. In a small bowl, combine the vinegar, oil, sugar, salt and a few grinds of pepper. Taste and adjust the flavor if you want it more sweet or sour.

In a large bowl, combine the green beans, chickpeas, kidney beans, celery and parsley. Add the dressing and toss. Refrigerate until ready to serve.

Irresistible Vegan Sandwiches, Wraps and Burgers

When I stopped eating meat, lunch became by far the most difficult meal of the day. Beyond peanut butter and jelly, it's hard to fathom a satisfying sandwich that you can easily pack up and take to work without some kind of sliced meat, lettuce and tomato.

Although I do still love peanut butter and jelly from time to time, I'm not a kid anymore. That's okay, because the recipes on the following pages prove that meals in a handheld package can be exciting and delicious even when composed entirely of vegetables.

Mediterranean Wraps with Vegan Tzatziki

Vegan yogurt can sometimes have an odd taste when eaten straight out of the container.
But when combined with cucumber, dill, garlic and lemon, it tastes exactly like regular tzatziki—
no one would ever guess that it's vegan! That's why soy yogurt has now replaced super expensive
cashews as my favorite base for creamy sauces and dips.

 Makes 4 wraps

1 medium cucumber

½ tsp plus a couple of pinches salt, divided

1 medium tomato, diced

¼ medium red onion, diced

¼ green bell pepper, seeded and diced

¼ cup (25 g) chopped black olives, preferably kalamata

2¼ cups (540 g) cooked chickpeas, or 1 (19-oz [540-g]) can, drained and rinsed

¾ cup (173 g) plain unsweetened vegan yogurt

2 tbsp (8 g) chopped fresh dill

1 clove garlic, minced

1 tbsp (15 ml) fresh lemon juice

Freshly ground black pepper

2 cups (110 g) chopped lettuce

4 large tortillas or wraps

Grate half of the cucumber and sprinkle it with a pinch of salt. Place it in a strainer over a bowl and let drain. Dice the other half of the cucumber.

In a bowl, combine the diced cucumber, tomato, red onion, bell pepper and black olives.

Put the chickpeas in a separate bowl and smash them with your hands or with a fork.

Squeeze as much water out of the grated cucumber as possible.

In a separate bowl, combine the grated cucumber, yogurt, dill, garlic, lemon juice and a pinch of salt and black pepper, to create the tzatziki.

Add 3 tablespoons (45 ml) of the tzatziki to the smashed chickpeas, along with ½ teaspoon of salt and black pepper to taste. Mix well.

Divide the lettuce among the 4 tortillas and top with the smashed chickpeas, mixed diced vegetables and a few dollops of tzatziki. Roll each up like a burrito.

If you like, you can toast the finished wraps in a dry skillet over medium-high heat. Start seam side down, to keep them from unwrapping, then carefully flip to the other side.

Bean and Rice Burritos with Easy Enchilada Sauce

Basic bean and rice burritos need no embellishments when the secret is in the sauce.
Who knew that such a delicious and spicy sauce was so simple to make at home?
You'll never buy bottled enchilada sauce again!

 Makes about 6 burritos

½ cup (100 g) uncooked white rice

1 cup (235 ml) plain tomato sauce

¼ cup (60 ml) vegetable stock

½ to 1 whole jalapeño pepper, or to taste

¼ medium onion, roughly chopped

2 cloves garlic, roughly chopped

½ tsp ground cumin

½ tsp dried oregano

½ tsp chili powder

¼ tsp salt

1½ cups (258 g) cooked black beans, or 1 (15.5-oz [439-g]) can, drained and rinsed

Juice of ½ lime

6 large tortillas

Baby spinach or other leafy greens

1 avocado, peeled, pitted and sliced

Put a small pot of water on to boil and cook the rice according to the package instructions. Drain when ready.

In a blender or small food processor, combine the tomato sauce, stock, jalapeño, onion, garlic, cumin, oregano, chili powder and salt and blend until smooth.

Transfer the sauce to a wide skillet and simmer over low heat for about 5 minutes, stirring regularly.

Add the beans and cooked rice to the sauce and mix well. Give it a couple of minutes on the stove to heat through. Remove from the heat and squeeze the lime juice over all. Give it one final mix.

Optional: Warm your tortillas wrapped in a dish towel in the microwave for a few seconds.

Put a small handful of spinach down the middle of each tortilla and top with the bean mixture and a couple of slices of avocado. Fold over the sides and roll it up from the bottom.

If you like, you can toast the finished burritos in a dry skillet over medium-high heat. Start seam side down, to keep them from unwrapping, then carefully flip to the other side.

Finger-Licking Peach BBQ Tempeh Sandwiches

Tempeh, like tofu, can be polarizing: you either love it or hate it. Also, as with tofu, you need to treat it right. Steaming your tempeh first helps to remove any bitter taste it may have and also improves its texture. Then, it's ready to be slathered in barbecue sauce! Use your favorite sauce, either store-bought or homemade; just make sure it's a good one!

 Serves 2 or 3

1 (8-oz [225-g]) package tempeh

½ cup (120 ml) water

¾ cup (188 g) barbecue sauce, divided

1 large peach

4 tsp (20 ml) oil, for pan, divided

1 tbsp (15 g) light or dark brown sugar

¼ cup (60 g) vegan mayonnaise

¼ cup packed (10 g) fresh basil

2 or 3 vegan sandwich buns

Salad greens or arugula

Cut the tempeh into 2 or 3 blocks and place it in a microwave-safe dish with a lid. Pour the water over the tempeh, making sure it all gets wet, though it doesn't have to be covered with water. Put the lid on the dish and microwave on high for 5 minutes. Alternatively, you can steam the tempeh for 10 minutes over a pot of boiling water on the stovetop, if you prefer.

Carefully remove the tempeh, cut it into ¾-inch (2-cm) cubes and place them into a bowl. Add ½ cup (125 g) of the barbecue sauce and stir to coat. Set aside to marinate for 15 minutes.

Meanwhile, prepare the peach by slicing it into ¼-inch (6-mm) rounds. Do this by slicing one side until you get to the pit, then turning it around and slicing from the other side until reaching the pit. Now, simply cut out the pit.

In a skillet, heat 1 teaspoon of the oil over medium-high heat. Sprinkle both sides of the peach slices with brown sugar and sear them for a couple of minutes on each side, or until they caramelize and are soft on the outside yet still firm on the inside. Transfer to a plate and set aside.

Make the basil mayo by pulsing the basil and mayonnaise together in a mini food processor or with an immersion blender in the tall cup that comes with it. If you don't have either of these tools, you can simply finely chop the basil and stir it into the mayonnaise.

In a large skillet, heat the remaining tablespoon (15 ml) of oil over medium heat. Transfer the tempeh and any sauce in the bottom of the bowl to the pan and fry, flipping the cubes as necessary, until browned and heated through, 7 to 10 minutes. If the pan becomes too dry, add a tablespoon or two of water. Stir through the remaining ¼ cup (63 g) of barbecue sauce and remove from the heat.

Build your sandwiches with a slather of basil mayo on each inner side of the bun, a handful of greens, a couple of slices of caramelized peaches and the BBQ tempeh. Serve immediately.

Black Bean Salsa Burgers

Salsa goes right in the burger patties rather than on top, to bring loads of flavor and texture to these plant-based burgers. Choose your favorite salsa; just be sure that it's really chunky. Straining the salsa to get just the flavorsome chunks prevents the burgers from being too wet and falling apart.

 Makes 4 or 5 burgers

2 tbsp (30 ml) oil, for pan, plus more for cooking burgers

1 small onion, diced

2 cloves garlic, finely chopped

1 cup (70 g) chopped button mushrooms (can be quite chunky as they will reduce when browned)

1 cup (80 g) rolled oats

1½ cups (258 g) cooked black beans, or 1 (15.5-oz [439-g]) can, drained and rinsed

1 cup (260 g) chunky salsa

1 tsp smoked paprika

1 tsp salt

Freshly ground black pepper

4 or 5 vegan hamburger buns

Your favorite hamburger fixings

If you're baking the burgers, preheat the oven to 375°F (190°C).

In a skillet, heat 1 tablespoon (15 ml) of the oil over medium-high heat. Add the onion and fry, stirring from time to time, for 5 to 7 minutes, or until soft and translucent, then add the garlic and fry for another 30 seconds, or until fragrant. Transfer to a large bowl.

Heat the remaining tablespoon (15 ml) of oil in the same skillet. Add the mushrooms and leave them for a minute to brown on one side before stirring and continuing to fry. Once browned all over, transfer to the bowl with the onion.

In a food processor, pulse the oats until you have mostly oat flour with some whole oats remaining, for texture. Transfer to the bowl. Put the black beans in the food processor and blend until mostly pureed with some whole beans remaining, also for texture. Transfer to the bowl.

Put the salsa in a strainer and stir to remove the excess tomato sauce, until you have mostly chunks remaining. Measure ½ cup (130 g) of this super chunky salsa and add it to the bowl along with the paprika, salt and pepper. Mix well to incorporate everything.

Form the mixture into 4 or 5 patties, depending on the size of your buns. The mix is a bit wet but should not be unmanageable. I take a ball in my hands, flatten it out into a patty on a plate, then use a spatula to transfer it to a baking pan or skillet when ready to cook. They may need a bit of reshaping once in the pan. If you're having trouble, you can add a bit more oat flour so that they hold together better.

To bake, lightly oil a baking pan, transfer the patties to the pan and bake for 20 minutes, flipping at 10 minutes. To fry, heat a large skillet over medium heat and add a tablespoon (15 ml) of oil. Fry the patties for 3 to 4 minutes per side, or until browned.

Once cooked, transfer the patties to a wire rack and let cool for a few minutes. They will firm up a bit as they cool. Serve on the buns with your favorite hamburger fixings.

10-Minute Curried Chickpea Wraps

Versatile chickpeas are definitely a favorite filling for cheap and hearty vegan sandwiches and wraps. These creamy curried chickpea wraps are deliciously spiced, easy and quick to throw together for a weekday lunch or a light dinner.

  Serves 4

⅔ cup (154 g) plain unsweetened vegan yogurt or vegan mayonnaise

2 tsp (4 g) curry powder, or to taste

½ tsp salt, or as necessary

½ tsp garlic powder

1 tbsp (15 ml) fresh lime juice

2¼ cups (540 g) cooked chickpeas, or 1 (19-oz [540-g]) can, drained and rinsed

1 medium carrot, julienned

½ medium cucumber, diced

1 medium tomato, diced

2 tbsp (5 g) chopped fresh cilantro

¼ medium red onion, diced

2 cups (110 g) chopped lettuce

4 large tortillas or wraps

In a small bowl, combine the yogurt, curry powder, salt, garlic powder and lime juice. Each curry powder is different, so add more if you need a little more curry flavor.

Put the chickpeas into a big bowl and mash them with a fork or squeeze them with your hands to break them up a bit. Add the carrot, cucumber, tomato, cilantro and onion, along with 4 tablespoons (60 ml) of the curry sauce and mix it up well.

Spread a portion of the lettuce down the center of each tortilla, top with the chickpea mixture and dollop over the remaining curry sauce. Fold the sides of the tortilla over the filling and roll it up from the bottom to close.

If you like, you can toast the finished wraps in a dry skillet over medium-high heat. Start seam side down, to keep them from unwrapping, then carefully flip to the other side.

Falafel Burgers

These burgers are quick to put together, but they do require some advanced planning.
Don't forget to put the dried chickpeas in a bowl of water to soak overnight. Don't be tempted to
cut corners and substitute canned or cooked chickpeas, as you will end up with mushy,
textureless burgers that lack the characteristic crunch of a delicious fried falafel.

 Makes 4 or 5 burgers

1 cup (211 g) dried chickpeas, soaked overnight

½ medium onion, roughly chopped

3 cloves garlic, roughly chopped

¼ cup packed (15 g) chopped fresh parsley

2 tsp (4 g) ground coriander

2 tsp (5 g) ground cumin

½ tsp chili powder

1 tsp salt

¼ tsp freshly ground black pepper

1 tbsp (8 g) all-purpose flour

2 tbsp (14 g) vegan breadcrumbs, or more as needed

1 tbsp (15 ml) oil, for pan

4 or 5 vegan hamburger buns

Your favorite hamburger fixings

Optional but recommended: vegan tzatziki sauce (page 99)

Drain the chickpeas and place them on a dish towel; pat and rub them dry. The drier they are, the better texture your burger will have. Transfer to a food processor along with the onion, garlic, parsley, coriander, cumin, chili powder, salt and pepper. Pulse the mixture until it has a mealy texture. Be careful not to overprocess it; you're not making hummus.

Transfer to a bowl, sprinkle with the flour and breadcrumbs and stir to incorporate them.

This burger mixture is not as sticky as other types of veggie burgers and they patties can be difficult to form by hand. The key to getting them to hold together is to use some kind of burger mold. No need to buy a special tool; you can use a 4-inch (10-cm) pastry ring or make one from tinfoil. To make a foil ring, simply fold a rectangle of tinfoil into a long strip, then form it into a 4-inch (10-cm) circle (or according to the size of your buns) and staple the ends together.

In a skillet, heat the oil over medium heat. Place your burger mold on a plate or cutting board and spoon in some of the chickpea mixture. Use the back of your spoon or the bottom of a glass to firmly pack down the burger mixture until you get a ½-inch (1.3-cm) thick patty; do not make them thicker. Slide off your mold and use a spatula to transfer the patty to the pan. Fry for 2 to 3 minutes, or until golden brown on the bottom. Gently flip it over and fry until golden brown on the other side.

Transfer to a plate and let cool for a couple of minutes to firm up.

Serve on buns with your favorite burger fixings and tzatziki sauce, if using.

Sweet Potato and Sauerkraut Sandwiches

I hope you love sauerkraut as much as I do because it's one of the best things ever. It's also really cheap and easy to make at home and a great way to use up leftover cabbage. I always keep a jar on hand to toss into sandwiches, salads, soup (yes, sauerkraut soup is a thing) or on a Buddha bowl.

 Makes 4 sandwiches

Sandwiches

1 large or 2 medium sweet potatoes (about 23 oz [640 g] total)

2 tbsp (30 ml) olive oil, plus more for pan

¾ tsp chili powder

½ tsp smoked paprika

¼ tsp garlic powder

Salt

Freshly ground black pepper

8 slices good-quality vegan bread

A couple of handfuls of lettuce or other leafy greens

1 cup (142 g) sauerkraut

2 tomatoes, sliced

Simple Thousand Island Dressing

½ cup (15 g) vegan mayonnaise

2 tbsp (30 g) ketchup

1 tsp white vinegar

¼ tsp garlic powder

¼ tsp onion powder

Salt, if necessary

Preheat the oven to 450°F (230°C).

Peel and slice the sweet potato from top to bottom into slabs about ½ inch (1.3 cm) thick. Place them on a lightly oiled baking sheet.

In a small bowl, mix together the oil, chili powder, smoked paprika and garlic powder. Brush this mixture over each side of the sweet potato slices and sprinkle with salt and pepper.

Place in the oven and roast (the oven does not need to be fully preheated to start roasting), flipping once, until tender, 15 to 20 minutes. Remove from the oven and let cool for a few minutes.

Meanwhile, prepare the dressing. In a small bowl, combine all of the dressing ingredients, taste and add salt if desired.

Toast the bread if desired.

Slather both inner sides of each pair of bread slices with the dressing and top with some lettuce, sweet potato, sauerkraut, tomatoes and any other of your favorite sandwich fixings.

Bee-Free Honey Mustard Chickpea Salad Sandwich

An easy twist on the typical chickpea salad sandwich is to whip up a simple sweet and tangy bee-free "honey" mustard dressing. You can enjoy this sandwich as is or you can pile on any extra veggies you might like.

 Makes 3 or 4 sandwiches

3 tbsp (42 g) vegan mayonnaise

1 tbsp (11 g) prepared yellow mustard

1 tbsp (15 ml) agave nectar or brown rice syrup

½ tsp white vinegar (optional)

1½ cups (360 g) cooked chickpeas, or 1 (15-oz [425-g] can, drained and rinsed

1 large or 2 small celery ribs, chopped

¼ medium red onion, diced

¼ tsp salt

Freshly ground black pepper

6 to 8 slices vegan bread

Salad greens

In a bowl, combine the mayonnaise, mustard and agave. Taste and adjust to your preference if you want it more sweet or mustardy. You can also add a bit of vinegar to cut through the sweetness, if you like.

Put the chickpeas in a bowl and mash with a fork. Add the dressing, celery, red onion, salt and pepper to taste.

Fill each sandwich with a small handful of salad greens and pile on the chickpea salad. This will make 3 or 4 sandwiches, depending on how much you stuff them and if you add any other sandwich fixings.

Smoky Tofu Banh Mi

I've said many times that banh mi is probably the world's most perfect sandwich. It's got the right balance of every flavor in a handheld package, and while it looks a bit complicated to make, it's actually pretty simple. The veggies here are quick-pickled, but if you have time, they can also be made ahead for even better flavor.

 Makes 4 sandwiches

Pickled Veggies

1 medium carrot

1 cup (116 g) sliced radishes (ideally daikon, but I usually use common red radishes)

½ cup (120 ml) rice, apple cider, or white wine vinegar

¼ cup (60 ml) water

2 tbsp (26 g) granulated sugar

1½ tsp (9 g) salt

Tofu

2 tbsp (30 ml) soy sauce

1½ tbsp (8 ml) water

1 tbsp (15 ml) pure maple syrup

1 tbsp (16 g) tomato paste

1½ tsp (8 g) light or dark brown sugar

¼ tsp garlic powder

1 (14-oz [400-g]) block extra-firm tofu

2 to 3 tbsp (16 to 24 g) cornstarch

1 tbsp (15 ml) oil, for pan

Banh Mi

2 tsp (10 ml) sriracha

½ cup (115 g) vegan mayonnaise

1 vegan baguette

½ small cucumber, sliced

Small bunch of cilantro

Start with the veggies, to give them time to pickle. Julienne the carrot (a julienne peeler makes quick work of this if you have one) and slice the radish. If using daikon, slice it into thick matchsticks; if using red radishes, slice them into rounds about ¼ inch (6 mm) thick.

In a small bowl, combine the vinegar, water, granulated sugar and salt and stir to dissolve the sugar. Pack a 1-quart (1-L) mason jar with the carrot and radish and pour in the pickling liquid. If it doesn't quite cover, add a touch more water. Refrigerate until ready to assemble your sandwiches.

To prepare the tofu, in a bowl, combine the soy sauce, water, maple syrup, tomato paste, brown sugar and garlic powder.

Drain the tofu and squeeze it between your hands over the sink get to the excess water out. Slice it into 6 slabs about ½ inch (1.3 cm) thick. Sprinkle 1 heaping tablespoon (about 8 to 12 g) of cornstarch into a large container, add the tofu in a single layer, then sprinkle with another heaping tablespoon (8 to 12 g) of cornstarch. Cover the container and shake to coat the tofu with cornstarch.

In a large nonstick skillet, heat the oil over medium-high heat. Add the tofu in a single layer and fry, flipping once, until crispy on both sides, about 2 minutes per side. Lower the heat to medium and pour in the sauce. Let the sauce simmer and thicken for a couple of minutes, flipping the tofu to coat it on both sides. Transfer the tofu to a plate.

Stir the sriracha into the mayo. Slice your baguette into 4 sandwich-size pieces and cut them open. You can remove a bit of the crumb to make more room for the filling, if you want.

Slather both inner halves of your bread with sriracha mayo. Add slices of cucumber and the tofu. Top with the pickled vegetables and fresh cilantro.

Serve immediately.

Savory
Small Bites

Are you the person that shows up to the party with a tub of hummus and a bag of chips? I can't tell you how many "bring something to share" parties I've been to where the snack table is composed entirely of hummus, guacamole, chips and raw vegetable sticks. Sometimes I think I only got invited because they know I'll actually bring something delicious (maybe I need new friends).

In this chapter, you'll find finger food and appetizer recipes that are great to share with guests at your next shindig as well as ideas for vegan snacks to curb your hunger when you can't make it till dinner.

My favorite are the Zoo Sticks with Ranch Dip (page 118), which remind me of some of my favorite pub fare but are also a great side dish for burgers instead of French fries. The Mini Vegan Spanish Omelet (page 121) is the perfect choice if you're hosting a tapas party. And you can never go wrong when you whip up the bean-packed Cowboy Caviar (page 137) and nachos.

Zoo Sticks with Ranch Dip

Zoo sticks, or zucchini fries, are an appetizer or snack that everyone is sure to love.
Especially when they're served with a vegan ranch dip that's good enough to drink. If you're a ranch
addict like myself, you can save yourself quite a bit of money by making your own vegan mayo.
My preferred method is to use aquafaba and oil, but there are many different methods
and simple recipes for vegan mayo available online.

 Serves 4

Zoo Sticks

Oil, for pan

2 medium zucchini

⅓ cup (41 g) all-purpose flour

½ cup (120 ml) unsweetened plant-based milk

1 cup (50 g) vegan panko or regular breadcrumbs

½ tsp salt

Freshly ground black pepper

Ranch Dip

¼ cup (60 g) vegan mayonnaise

¼ cup (60 g) plain unsweetened vegan yogurt

½ tsp dried dill

½ tsp dried parsley

¼ tsp garlic powder

¼ tsp onion powder

⅛ tsp salt

Freshly ground black pepper

Preheat the oven to 475°F (245°C), line a baking pan with foil and lightly oil.

Slice the zucchini in half widthwise. Cut each piece from top to bottom into quarters and then cut those quarters lengthwise in half again. You should end up with 16 spears from each zucchini.

Place the flour and milk in 2 separate bowls. In a third shallow bowl, combine the breadcrumbs with the salt and pepper.

Roll each zucchini spear in the flour, shaking off the excess, then dip them into the milk and finally roll in the breadcrumbs, pressing them in so that they stick.

Place the spears on the prepared baking pan and bake for 15 minutes, flipping halfway through, until lightly golden brown and crispy on the outside and tender on the inside.

Meanwhile, prepare the ranch dip: In a bowl, combine all the dip ingredients.

Let the zoo sticks cool for a couple of minutes, then serve with the ranch dip.

Zoo sticks are best eaten fresh, as they will lose their crispiness as they cool.

Mini Vegan Spanish Omelet

This Spanish omelet, *tortilla de patatas*, is a bit smaller than those you'd find in a Spanish tapas bar. This is for you to be able to fry the potatoes in just one batch rather than the two or three that it normally takes. This size is perfect for a snack or tapas dish with a cold beer. Make note of the pan size I use to get a well-proportioned tortilla.

 Serves 4 as a tapa

½ cup (60 g) chickpea (garbanzo) flour
½ cup (120 ml) water
Oil, for frying
½ small onion, finely diced
½ tsp salt
Freshly ground black pepper
1½ cups (about 7.5 oz) peeled and sliced potatoes (sliced into half moons about ¼" [6 mm] thick)

In a large bowl, combine the chickpea flour and water and stir until mostly mixed. There will still be some lumps but that's okay for now. Set aside.

In a large nonstick pan, heat 1 tablespoon (15 ml) of oil over medium-high heat. Fry the onion until tender, 5 to 7 minutes. Use a slotted spoon to transfer it from the pan to a plate.

Add enough oil to your pan to fill to a ¼-inch (6-mm) depth and allow it to heat up. I usually test the heat of my oil by inserting a wooden chopstick. When the oil bubbles up around the chopstick, it's hot enough. Add the potatoes to the pan, arranging them in a single layer, if you can. Fry until tender, about 5 minutes, stirring from time to time so that they don't stick to the bottom of the pan. You don't need to brown the potatoes, just fry until they are tender all the way through.

Meanwhile, stir your garbanzo flour batter to get out all the lumps. Add the salt, pepper and fried onions. When the potatoes are tender, use a slotted spoon to remove the potatoes from the oil and add them to the batter.

Heat a 6-inch (15-cm) nonstick pan over medium heat and add ½ teaspoon of oil. Swirl the oil around the pan and up the sides so that it is well coated.

Stir your batter so that the potatoes and onions are evenly distributed, and pour it all into the small pan. Smooth over the top with a spoon. Allow to cook for 6 to 7 minutes, or until the top is mostly set and the sides are beginning to turn golden brown. You can check them by gently sliding a spatula down the side of the pan and taking a peek.

Now the fun part: Put a plate over the pan and, in one motion, flip the pan over so that the tortilla falls onto the plate. Use your spatula to gently slide the tortilla back into the pan. Gently reshape the sides of the tortilla with your spatula to form the tortilla shape you see in the picture. Cook for an additional 5 minutes on this side.

Flip the tortilla back onto the plate. Serve either sliced into wedges like a pie or cubed to pick up with toothpicks. Spanish omelets can be eaten hot or cold.

Mediterranean Stuffed Mushrooms

These delightful mushrooms have a creamy filling with a distinctly cheesy taste, thanks to the nutritional yeast. You may not be able to find nutritional yeast in every grocery store, but it is often available in bulk food stores and online (where you'll get the best price). These make a great appetizer for when you're having guests over—they may not believe that they're vegan!

 Makes 12 mushrooms

12 large white mushrooms
5 tsp (25 ml) olive oil, divided, plus more for brushing and pan
¼ cup (40 g) chopped red onion
2 cloves garlic, minced
1 (14-oz [400-g]) can artichoke hearts
¼ cup (32 g) nutritional yeast
2 tbsp (5 g) chopped fresh basil or parsley
¼ cup (60 g) vegan mayonnaise
¼ cup (28 g) vegan breadcrumbs
½ tsp salt, plus more for sprinkling
Freshly ground black pepper

Preheat the oven to 375°F (190°C).

If any of your mushrooms are dirty, gently brush them off with a damp towel. Remove and roughly chop the stems if they're clean.

In a medium pan, heat 1½ teaspoons (8 ml) of the oil over medium-high heat and sauté the onion until soft and translucent, 5 to 7 minutes. Add the garlic and sauté for 30 seconds to 1 minute more, or until fragrant. Transfer to a large bowl.

Add another 1½ teaspoons (8 ml) of the oil to the pan along with the chopped mushroom stems. Leave them to fry and brown on the first side for about 2 minutes, then give them a stir and continue to fry. Once they're browned all over, transfer them to the bowl with the onion.

Drain the artichoke hearts and roughly chop them. Add them to the bowl along with the nutritional yeast and basil. Stir everything together and let cool for about 5 minutes before adding the mayonnaise or else it will melt.

Meanwhile, in a small bowl, combine the breadcrumbs with the remaining 2 teaspoons (10 ml) of olive oil. Mix and mash together well.

Lightly oil a baking pan and place the mushroom caps on it, stem end up. Sprinkle a bit of salt and pepper inside each cap. If you want, you can brush a bit of olive oil on the mushroom caps.

Stir the mayonnaise, salt and a generous grind of pepper into the artichoke mixture. Taste and adjust the seasoning if you think it's necessary. Use a small spoon to fill the mushroom caps with the mixture, packing it in and mounding it on top. Top with a spoonful of the breadcrumbs and press them into the filling.

Bake for 12 to 15 minutes, depending on the size of the mushrooms, or until the breadcrumbs are golden brown and the filling is heated through. If they are slow to brown on top, pop them under the broiler for a few minutes, watching carefully. Serve warm.

Mexican Tortilla Pinwheels

Tortilla pinwheels are a fun finger food to serve at parties. The black bean and salsa filling in these pinwheels is delicious enough to serve as a stand-alone dip, if you prefer.

 Serves 6 to 8

3 cups (516 g) cooked black beans, or 2 (15.5-oz [439-g]) cans, drained and rinsed

¾ cup (260 g) salsa

2 tsp (10 ml) fresh lime juice

¼ tsp ground cumin

¼ tsp smoked paprika

¼ cup (10 g) roughly chopped fresh cilantro

¼ cup (40 g) finely diced red onion

¼ cup (38 g) seeded and finely diced red bell pepper

¼ cup (37 g) finely diced avocado

½ to 1 tsp salt

4 large tortillas or wraps

In a blender or food processor, combine the beans, salsa, lime juice, cumin and smoked paprika and blend until you reach an almost smooth consistency with some bean chunks remaining for texture.

Transfer to a bowl and mix in the cilantro, red onion, bell pepper and avocado. Add salt to taste (it depends on how salty your beans and salsa are).

Spread one-quarter of the mixture over each tortilla, stopping 1 inch (2.5 cm) from one end of the tortilla. Roll it up tightly toward and against the bare edge.

You can slice it into rounds and serve immediately or wrap each tortilla roll in plastic wrap and refrigerate for a couple of hours. I don't like to refrigerate them for longer than that, or the tortillas can start to get a bit soggy.

Buffalo Chickpea Stuffed Potatoes

These stuffed potatoes are great for when you need a small snack and crave something spicy. No need to turn on the oven to bake a potato; they do just fine in the microwave. The chickpeas swim in a spicy tomato sauce that's perfect for spooning over potatoes.

  Serves 2

2 medium baking potatoes

¼ cup plus 2 tbsp (90 ml) tomato sauce

½ cup plus 2 tbsp (150 ml) buffalo sauce, or more to taste

1½ cups (360 g) cooked chickpeas, or 1 (15-oz [425-g]) can, drained and rinsed

Salt

Freshly ground black pepper

Optional for serving: vegan butter, vegan ranch dip (page 118), plain vegan yogurt or vegan sour cream, a sprinkling of your favorite chopped fresh herb or green onion, diced avocado

Prick the potatoes all over with a fork and place them on a microwave-safe plate. Microwave on high until they are soft and easily pierced with a knife, about 10 minutes, turning them over halfway through.

Meanwhile, prepare the chickpeas. In a large saucepan, combine the tomato sauce, buffalo sauce and chickpeas over medium-low heat. Simmer gently until the sauce is thick and the chickpeas are heated through, about 5 minutes. Taste and add more buffalo sauce if you want them spicier.

Slice open the potatoes and gently fluff the insides with a fork. Sprinkle generously with salt and pepper and a slathering of vegan butter, if desired. Top with the buffalo chickpeas and your choice of optional toppings.

Guacamole Potato Skins

There can never be enough ways to eat guacamole. Or potatoes. So, these crispy potato skins topped with creamy, rich guacamole are the perfect finger food. Yes, avocados can be expensive, but if you stock up when they're on sale, you can freeze them. Frozen avocados are perfect for guacamole!

 Serves 4 to 6

10 baby potatoes

1 large avocado

1 clove garlic, minced

2 tbsp (20 g) finely diced red onion

½ medium Roma tomato, seeded and finely diced

1 tbsp (3 g) chopped fresh cilantro

1½ tbsp (23 ml) fresh lime juice

1 tsp salt, divided

Freshly ground black pepper

1¼ tsp (12 ml) olive oil

Optional for serving: vegan ranch dip (page 118), vegan sour cream or plain vegan yogurt, salsa

Slice the potatoes in half and place, cut side down, on a microwave-safe plate. Microwave on high in 2-minute intervals until they can be easily pierced with a knife, 5 to 6 minutes. Let cool for a few minutes.

Meanwhile, make the guacamole. In a medium bowl, mash the avocado and mix it with the garlic, onion, tomato, cilantro, lime juice, ½ teaspoon of the salt and pepper to taste.

Preheat the broiler.

Use a small spoon to carefully scoop out the potato insides, leaving about ¼ inch (6 mm) of the flesh. Brush both sides with oil and sprinkle with the remaining ½ teaspoon of salt and pepper. Place, cut side down, on a baking pan and broil for 5 to 10 minutes, or until crispy, then flip them and broil for a few minutes more until the skin is crispy.

Let them cool for a few minutes, then stuff with guacamole and your choice of additions.

Serve immediately while the skins are still crispy—they soften as they cool.

> **Note:** You can save the removed potato flesh in an airtight container to serve as a side to your lunch or dinner another day. I love potatoes, so I usually end up eating it while I'm making the potato skins!

Rainbow Thai Curry Peanut Kebabs

Ready for a little grilling? These colorful grilled veggie kebabs will be a hit with anyone who tries them. They're packed with flavor, thanks to a healthy brushing of spicy Thai curry peanut sauce while grilling—and more to serve on the side!

 Serves 4 to 6

Kebabs

½ medium red bell pepper, seeded and cut into 12 chunks

½ zucchini, cut into 1" (2.5-cm) half-moons

¼ red onion, cut into chunks

12 small button mushrooms, cleaned and stemmed

12 cherry tomatoes

1 tbsp (15 ml) olive oil

½ tsp salt

Freshly ground black pepper

Curry Peanut Sauce

¼ cup (65 g) natural peanut butter

1½ tsp (3 g) minced fresh ginger

1 clove garlic, minced

1½ tbsp (23 ml) soy sauce

1 tbsp (15 g) light brown sugar

1 tbsp (15 ml) fresh lime juice

1 to 2 tsp (15 to 30 g) vegan Thai red curry paste

3 tbsp (45 ml) warm water

You will need twelve 6-inch (15-cm) skewers. If using wooden skewers and you are putting these on a barbecue (as opposed to a grill pan), soak them in water for 20 to 30 minutes beforehand so that they don't burn.

For the kebabs, place all the chopped veggies in a bowl, drizzle with the olive oil and sprinkle with salt and pepper to taste. Toss with your hands to ensure they are well coated.

To prepare the sauce, in a small bowl, stir together all the sauce ingredients, adding as much curry paste as you like for spice.

Thread the veggies onto the skewers, one of each veggie per skewer, leaving a bit of space between each veggie so that they cook evenly.

Heat a lightly oiled grill pan over medium-high heat. Grill the kebabs for 7 to 10 minutes, turning several times and brushing with the peanut sauce after each turn, until the veggies are soft and have char marks around the edges.

Serve with the remaining peanut sauce on the side to dip.

Summery Tomato Pesto Tarts

An easy summer appetizer for when basil and tomatoes are at their peak,
these puff pastry tarts are perfect for pesto lovers. Many brands of puff pastry are vegan,
but be sure to double-check the ingredients.

 Makes 6 tarts

1 cup (40 g) packed fresh basil

¼ cup (30 g) roughly chopped walnuts

1 tbsp (15 ml) fresh lemon juice

1 clove garlic, roughly chopped

2 tbsp (16 g) nutritional yeast

2 tbsp (30 ml) olive oil, plus more for tart

½ tsp salt, plus more for tart

1 large heirloom or beefsteak tomato

1 sheet vegan puff pastry, thawed according to the package directions

Freshly ground black pepper

Preheat the oven to 400°F (200°C).

In a small food processor, combine most of the basil, reserving some small leaves for garnish, and the walnuts, lemon juice, garlic, nutritional yeast, olive oil and salt and process until blended. Thinly slice the tomato.

Unfold the puff pastry. Gently roll out the puff pastry on a lightly floured counter to a 10 x 12-inch (25 x 20-cm) rectangle. Cut the pastry into 6 rectangles. Gently score a ¼-inch (6-mm) border around each rectangle and poke the interior of the rectangle 3 or 4 times with a fork.

Spread some pesto inside each rectangle, avoiding the scored borders (see Note). Place a slice of tomato on each rectangle and lightly brush the tomato with olive oil and sprinkle with salt and pepper. Bake for 15 to 20 minutes, or until the crust is puffy and golden brown.

Cool the tarts for 5 minutes, then sprinkle with the reserved basil leaves and drizzle with a touch more olive oil, if desired.

Note: You might have some pesto left over. Store it in an airtight container in the fridge for a sandwich, or freeze it to add to a vegetable soup another day.

Single-Serving Pita Pizzas

Using pita bread as a pizza crust is a quick, no-fuss way to fulfill your sudden pizza cravings.
The key to a delicious vegan pizza without resorting to expensive vegan cheese is to really pack on
the veggies. If you're one of those weirdos, like me, who likes ranch with pizza,
you'll find a recipe for vegan ranch dip on page 118.

 Serves 4

4 pitas

¼ cup (60 ml) tomato sauce

⅛ tsp Italian seasoning

Salt

Freshly ground black pepper

¼ cup (40 g) finely diced onion

¼ cup (38 g) seeded and finely diced
green bell pepper

8 black olives, sliced

8 cherry tomatoes, sliced

Optional: any of your other favorite
vegan pizza toppings

Optional for serving: a sprinkling of
red pepper flakes, olive oil, vegan
ranch dip (page 118)

Preheat the oven to 425°F (220°C).

Place the pitas on a baking pan and divide the tomato sauce equally among
them. Sprinkle with a pinch of Italian seasoning, salt and pepper.

Divide the toppings among the pita pizzas and bake for 10 to 15 minutes, or
until the pitas are golden brown and the toppings are soft. The oven does not
have to be totally preheated when you put them in.

Serve with a sprinkling of red pepper flakes, a drizzling of olive oil and vegan
ranch dressing, if desired.

Cowboy Caviar

If you've never had cowboy caviar before, a bean-based dip might seem a bit odd. In fact, this hearty and refreshing mix of beans and veggies tossed in a tangy dressing is highly addictive after just one bite. Once you taste it, you'll get it!

 Serves 6

1½ cups (258 g) cooked black beans, or 1 (15.5-oz [439-g]) can, drained and rinsed

1½ cups (248 g) cooked black-eyed peas, or 1 (15-oz [425-g]) can, drained and rinsed

1 cup (150 g) canned or frozen corn (thawed if frozen)

1 cup (150 g) seeded and diced red bell pepper

½ medium red onion, diced

1 cup (180 g) diced Roma tomatoes (2 to 3 tomatoes)

¾ cup (30 g) chopped fresh cilantro

1 jalapeño pepper, diced

¼ cup (60 ml) olive oil

¼ cup (60 ml) red or white wine vinegar

½ tsp chili powder

½ tsp ground cumin

½ tsp smoked paprika

¼ tsp garlic powder

½ tsp salt, or more to taste

Freshly ground black pepper

1 (7-oz [200-g]) bag vegan nacho chips

In a large bowl, combine the black beans, black-eyed peas, corn, bell pepper, onion, tomatoes, cilantro and jalapeño.

In a mason jar, combine the remaining ingredients, except the chips, cover with the lid, and shake it up.

Pour the dressing over the bean mixture and toss to combine. Taste and add more salt, if necessary—remember, the nacho chips are salty, too.

Serve immediately with the nacho chips or refrigerate until later. Keep in mind that the veggies will release some liquid if you choose to serve it later; just give it a stir before serving.

Quick and Easy Morning Munchies

So, what do vegans eat for breakfast? Judging from Instagram, it must be smoothie bowls and chia. Well, grab your cup of coffee and flip through this chapter because, whether you're a sweet or a savory breakfast kind of person, there's a delicious plant-based morning munchie recipe here for you!

If you've been mourning the loss of eggs in your diet, then check out my Mini Quiche Cups (page 140). They make use of my favorite egg replacer, chickpea flour, to make a veggie-packed grab-and-go breakfast that's perfect for busy mornings. Instead of avocado toast (avocados are expensive!), try Blistered Cherry Tomatoes and Beans on Garlic Toast (page 144). And if you're craving something über-quick and sweet, Sweet and Simple Broiled Grapefruit (page 159) is where it's at!

Mini Quiche Cups

These mini quiche cups are a great grab-and-go breakfast. They are equally delicious fresh out of the oven as they are served cold. One pan will last you for breakfasts all week and you can also freeze them for later.

 Makes 12 quiches

1 tbsp (15 ml) oil, for skillet, plus more for muffin tin

1½ cups (180 g) chickpea (garbanzo) flour

1½ cups (355 ml) water

1 tsp baking powder

2 tsp (12 g) salt, plus a pinch for the vegetables

Freshly ground black pepper

3 cups (285 g) small-diced mixed frozen veggies

Preheat the oven to 425°F (220°C) and coat a 12-well muffin tin with oil.

In a large bowl, stir together the flour, water, baking powder, salt and pepper. The batter will still be quite lumpy at this point, which is fine; just set it aside while you prepare the veggies.

In a large skillet, heat the tablespoon (15 ml) of oil over medium heat. Add the frozen vegetables and allow them to fry, undisturbed, for a couple of minutes, then toss. Continue to fry until heated through and beginning to brown. Keep in mind that frozen veggies are already parcooked, so they may cook twice as fast as fresh vegetables. Season with a pinch of salt.

Give the batter another whisk and try to get most of the remaining lumps out. Add the veggies to the batter and fill the prepared muffin tin with the batter. You can fill each well up to the top and make sure each has a good helping of veggies.

Bake for 15 minutes, or until the tops are set and a toothpick inserted into the center of a quiche comes out clean—it might have some crumbs on it, but it shouldn't be wet.

Let cool in the tin for 5 minutes, then pop them out to cool on a wire rack.

Basic Buttermilk Pancakes

These pancakes are fluffy and tender with a delicious tang from the vegan buttermilk.
I tried several different kinds of plant-based milk to make buttermilk and found that soy milk
thickened the best, so it's what I recommend here. These pancakes are so good that
no one will believe that they're dairy- and egg-free!

 Makes 6 to 8 pancakes

1 tbsp (15 ml) apple cider vinegar

1 scant cup (220 ml) unsweetened soy milk

1 cup (125 g) all-purpose flour

1 tbsp (14 g) baking powder

2 tbsp (26 g) sugar

¼ tsp salt

1½ tbsp (23 ml) melted vegan butter, plus more for pan

Your favorite pancake toppings, such as pure maple syrup, jam, berries in syrup (page 156), bananas foster (page 178)

Put the vinegar into a measuring cup. Add the soy milk until you reach the 1-cup (235-ml) mark. Set aside.

In a large bowl, combine the flour, baking powder, sugar and salt.

Start heating a pan over medium heat. Lightly grease with vegan butter.

When the pan is ready to go, stir the melted vegan butter into the soy milk, then pour it all into the bowl of dry ingredients. Mix until just combined. It's okay if it is still a bit lumpy. Overmixing will make your pancakes flat!

Measure out ¼ cup (60 ml) of the batter and pour it into the pan. Cook for a couple of minutes, until bubbles appear on the surface and the bottom is golden brown. Flip and cook on the other side until golden brown. Transfer to a plate and continue with the rest of the batter. You may need to add a bit more vegan butter from time to time and adjust the heat if they start browning too quickly.

Serve immediately with your favorite pancake toppings.

Blistered Cherry Tomatoes and Beans on Garlic Toast

If you're an avocado toast kind of person but can't afford your daily avocado habit,
try beans on toast instead. My nickname for this dish is "posh beans on toast"
and it's one of my favorite recipes, as it's so simple yet flavorful.

 Serves 2 to 4

1 tbsp (15 ml) oil, for pan, plus more for drizzling

¼ medium red onion, diced

10 oz (275 g) cherry tomatoes (25 to 30 tomatoes)

1½ cups (270 g) cooked white beans, or 1 (15-oz [425-g]) can, drained and rinsed

1 tbsp (15 ml) balsamic vinegar

½ tsp salt, plus more to taste

Freshly ground black pepper

4 thick slices good-quality vegan bread

1 small clove garlic

3 tbsp (8 g) chopped fresh basil or parsley

In a large skillet, heat the oil over medium-high heat. Add the onion and sauté until soft and transparent, 5 to 7 minutes. Add the cherry tomatoes and leave them for a few minutes without stirring, until they begin to crack open on the bottom and release their juices. Give them a stir and continue to cook until they are soft and cracked all over.

Stir in the beans, vinegar, salt and pepper to taste. Cook until the beans are heated through, a minute or two, stirring gently from time to time. Don't overcook or stir too vigorously, as they'll start to break down into mush.

Meanwhile, toast the bread. Rub the clove of garlic over each piece of toast.

Spoon the bean mixture over each piece of garlic toast, sprinkle with some chopped basil and drizzle with olive oil. Season with additional salt and pepper, if necessary.

Spring Vegetable Crepes

I'm not going to lie, it took me a couple of attempts to learn how to get perfectly formed crepes each time. The good thing is that these vegan crepes taste just like traditional ones and can be used for both sweet and savory fillings.

 Makes 4 large or 6 medium crepes

Filling

1 to 2 tbsp (15 to 30 ml) olive oil, for pan, divided

1 small onion, diced

2 cloves garlic, minced

Salt

Freshly ground black pepper

12 oz (350 g) any variety of mushrooms, sliced (about 4 cups)

1 bunch asparagus (15 to 18 medium spears), woody ends discarded, chopped

Crepes

1¼ cups (285 ml) unsweetened plant-based milk

2½ tbsp (38 ml) olive oil, plus more for pan

1 cup (125 g) all-purpose flour

½ tsp sugar

½ tsp salt

½ tsp baking powder

⅔ cup (164 g) of your favorite hummus (I use roasted beet hummus)

Optional: your favorite chopped fresh herb, a handful of leafy greens

In a large skillet, heat 1 tablespoon (15 ml) of the oil over medium-high heat. Add the onion and garlic and season with a pinch of salt and pepper. Sauté for about 5 minutes, or until softened, then add the mushrooms. Leave the mushrooms untouched to brown on the first side for a minute or two, then stir and brown on the other side. Season with a pinch of salt and pepper and transfer to a plate.

Lower the heat to medium. If the pan is dry, you can add the remaining tablespoon (15 ml) of oil. Add the asparagus to the pan and season with a pinch of salt and pepper. Sauté for a couple of minutes, until bright green and crisp-tender. Transfer to the plate with the mushrooms and cover to keep warm.

To prepare the crepes, in a large bowl, combine the plant-based milk and oil. Sift in the flour, sugar, salt and baking powder. Whisk well to get out most of the lumps.

My pan measures 7 inches (18 cm) across the bottom and I use between ¼ and ⅓ cup (60 and 80 ml) of batter per crepe. You can use a larger or smaller pan; just adjust the amount of batter accordingly. Oil your pan with a very thin layer of oil and heat over medium heat. Holding the pan off the heat in one hand, pour the batter directly into the middle of the pan and begin swirling the pan to distribute the batter in a thin layer all the way to the edges. Fry for about a minute, or until the edges are golden brown. Carefully slide a spatula under and around the entire edge of the crepe to release it before sliding your spatula under the middle and flipping the crepe over. Fry for an additional 30 seconds to 1 minute, or until golden brown. Transfer to a plate and cover with a tea towel to keep warm.

Note that the first crepe usually comes out wonky, so don't get discouraged if that happens. There is enough batter to make six 7-inch (18-cm) crepes plus 1 wonky one. Also note that you may need to add a bit more oil to the pan if they start to stick and to lower the heat after the first couple of crepes as the pan heats up.

Spread about 1½ tablespoons (23 g) of hummus down the middle of each crepe and top with the filling mixture. Feel free to add a small handful of leafy greens or a sprinkling of your favorite herb. Fold the crepes over and serve.

Gingerbread Oatmeal

The first time I tasted this, I was genuinely surprised by how much it actually tastes like gingerbread. This combination of spices and molasses is unmistakable. Oats have always been a cheap breakfast staple, and if you're looking to up your oatmeal game by trying out some new flavors, this one should be next on your list.

 Serves 1

½ cup (40 g) rolled oats

1 cup (235 ml) plant-based milk, plus ¼ cup (60 ml) to serve

¼ tsp ground ginger

¼ tsp ground cinnamon

⅛ tsp salt

1½ tsp (8 ml) molasses

2 tsp (10 g) dark brown sugar

Optional toppings: walnuts or pecans, dried raisins or cranberries, sliced banana

In a small saucepan over medium heat, stir together all of the ingredients, except the ¼ cup (60 ml) of plant-based milk. Bring to a simmer and stir continuously until the oats are tender and the liquid is absorbed, about 5 minutes.

Serve in a bowl and drizzle with the remaining ¼ cup (60 ml) of milk and any additional toppings of your choice.

Cranberry-Oat Breakfast Cookies

Bet you can't eat just one of these soft and chewy cookies. They're great to take for breakfast, but you're sure to be snacking on them all throughout the day as well!

 Makes about 10 cookies

½ cup (63 g) all-purpose flour
1½ cups (120 g) quick oats
½ cup (100 g) sugar
1 tsp baking powder
¼ tsp salt
¾ cup (90 g) dried cranberries
3 tbsp (26 g) pumpkin seeds
4 tbsp (60 ml) vegan butter, melted
½ cup (120 ml) plant-based milk

Preheat the oven to 375°F (190°C) and line a baking sheet with parchment paper.

In a large bowl, combine the flour, oats, sugar, baking powder, salt, cranberries and pumpkin seeds.

When the oven is heated, add the melted vegan butter and plant-based milk to the dry ingredients and mix well.

Form the dough into balls. You can use a cookie or ice cream scoop, but I just get in there with my hands and press the dough together into balls. You can make them as big or small as you like. I generally get about 10 cookies from this recipe.

Place the balls on the prepared baking sheet and gently flatten them with the palm of your hand.

Bake for 20 minutes, or until they no longer appear wet on top and the bottoms are beginning to turn golden brown. They will brown a bit on top, but not as much as other cookies, so it's better to judge by dryness rather than color.

Remove from the oven and let cool on the pan.

Sweet Potato and Black Bean Breakfast Burritos

For those of us who are more savory than sweet breakfast people, thank goodness someone invented breakfast burritos. The best thing about breakfast burritos is that they can be wrapped in tinfoil and frozen to take throughout the week. Simply unwrap them and defrost in the microwave.

 Makes 5 or 6 burritos

2 medium-large sweet potatoes

½ cup (115 g) plain unsweetened vegan yogurt

2¼ tsp (6 g) taco seasoning

6 large flour or whole wheat tortillas

1½ cups (258 g) cooked black beans, or 1 (15.5-oz [439-g]) can, drained and rinsed

Salt

Freshly ground black pepper

Optional: sliced avocado, baby spinach or other leafy green, a few drops of hot sauce, fresh cilantro, squeeze of lime

Poke holes all over the sweet potato and microwave on high for 10 to 15 minutes, turning at about the 7-minute point, until they can be easily pierced with a knife. The cooking time will depend on how fat your sweet potatoes are.

When they're soft, slice them in half and let them cool for a few minutes. If you're making these to freeze, let the sweet potato cool completely. You can put it in the fridge to speed it up.

Meanwhile, in a small bowl, stir together the yogurt and taco seasoning.

Scoop the flesh out of the sweet potatoes and transfer to a separate bowl. Smash with a fork and add salt and pepper to taste.

If your tortillas are cold and you think they'll crack when wrapping, warm them, wrapped in a tea towel, in the microwave for a few seconds.

Spread a small amount of sweet potato puree down the middle of a tortilla, top with black beans, any optional toppings and a drizzle of the seasoned yogurt. If freezing, choose your optional toppings carefully. Avocado is not good thawed in the microwave! Fold the left and right sides over and roll it up from the bottom.

Before serving, toast the burritos in a dry skillet over medium heat for a couple of minutes on each side, if you wish.

To freeze, wrap the burritos tightly in tinfoil. To thaw, remove the tinfoil and microwave on high for 2 to 3 minutes, or until heated through.

5-Minute Granola

Granola in the microwave, you say? What kind of sorcery is this? Yes, forget about your expensive store-bought granola, as it's one of the unexpected things you can make from scratch, using just your microwave. Try it!

 Serves 1

½ cup (40 g) rolled oats

¼ cup (30 g) chopped nuts of your choice

1½ tbsp (23 ml) brown rice syrup, agave nectar or pure maple syrup

1½ tbsp (23 ml) neutral oil, coconut oil or vegan butter

⅛ tsp ground cinnamon

¼ cup (35 g) dried fruit of your choice (raisins, cranberries, cherries, etc.)

In a microwave-safe bowl, combine all of the ingredients, except the dried fruit. If using solid coconut oil or vegan butter, cut it into pieces and dot over the top.

Microwave on high for 2 minutes, stopping and stirring at the 1-minute mark; the oats should be toasty and golden brown. If they are not toasty enough for you, you can continue microwaving and stirring in 30-second intervals. Don't go too far, though, or the granola will burn.

Remove from the microwave and stir in the dried fruit. Spread the granola onto a plate and press it down with the back of your spoon or a spatula. This is to help it stick together into clumps—in my tests, I found that brown rice syrup and agave had superior clumping properties over maple syrup, but it will still taste delicious even if not clumpy.

Let cool for 5 to 10 minutes, or until crunchy.

Fruity Granola Yogurt Parfait

This pretty parfait has all the elements of a delicious breakfast, but could also double as an easy dessert! You can use one berry or a mix, or replace the frozen berries for fresh when they're in season.

 Makes 2 parfaits

Berries in Syrup

2 cups (310 g) frozen berries (your favorite berry or a mixture)

2 tbsp (30 ml) water

2 tbsp (26 g) sugar, or more to taste

2 tsp (5 g) cornstarch

1 cup (230 g) vegan yogurt

1 recipe 5-Minute Granola (page 155)

Optional toppings: a drizzle of agave nectar, pure maple syrup, brown rice syrup, your favorite fresh herb or shaved chocolate

In a small saucepan, combine the berries, water, sugar and cornstarch over medium heat and mix well. Bring to a simmer and cook, stirring, until thickened, about 3 minutes. Lower the heat to low and continue to cook until the berries are thawed and hot throughout, about another 3 minutes. Remove from the heat and let cool for a couple of minutes. Taste, and if you want them sweeter, now is your chance to add more sugar.

Spoon 2 to 3 tablespoons (30 to 45 g) of the yogurt into the bottom of a glass. If you want, you can add a drizzle of liquid sweetener over the yogurt. Top with a layer of granola, then a layer of berries. Repeat the layers until you get to the top. Serve with your choice of additional toppings.

Sweet and Simple Broiled Grapefruit

Grapefruit season is during the winter, which is why so many remember their mom making broiled grapefruit for them at Christmas. You can make it anytime you want, though; it's simple and takes less than 10 minutes.

 Serves 1 or 2

1 grapefruit

2 tbsp (30 g) dark brown sugar or (30 ml) pure maple syrup

Optional: a sprinkling of ground cinnamon, a few leaves of mint, vegan whipped cream

Preheat the broiler and line a baking pan with tinfoil.

Slice the grapefruit in half and use a sharp knife to cut around the grapefruit, between the flesh and the rind. Then, cut between each segment. You don't want to remove the segments, just loosen them so that they're easier to scoop out with a spoon.

Place the grapefruit on the pan and sprinkle each cut half with 1 tablespoon (15 g) of the brown sugar. You can also add a sprinkling of cinnamon, if you want.

Broil for about 4 minutes, or until the sugar is bubbly and beginning to caramelize.

Remove from the broiler and let cool for a couple of minutes. Just before serving, garnish with mint or vegan whipped cream, if desired.

Snappy Sweet Treats

Have you ever needed a dessert nice enough to serve to guests but don't have time to freeze that no-bake raw vegan layered blueberry cheesecake overnight? Has your sweet tooth suddenly decided that it needs something NOW and a piece of fruit just isn't going to cut it?

In this chapter, you'll find a variety of delectable and cashew-less desserts and sweet treats that are ready in no time. If you're a fruit-based dessert lover, check out the Apple Crumble for One (or More) (page 162). Although it's cooked in the microwave, you'd never know the difference between that and a crumble that's been baked for 45 minutes. For chocolate lovers, you have Effortless Chocolate-Covered Stuffed Dates (page 173), which are just like a box of vegan chocolates!

Apple Crumble for One (or More)

There's nothing sadder than a soggy crumble. Unfortunately, that sometimes happens when you bake the crumble right on top of the filling. This recipe takes care of that by toasting the crumble in a pan while the filling is cooking. This single-serving crumble is perfect for those days you're craving something sweet but don't want to make a whole pan.

 Serves 1

Filling

1 Granny Smith apple

1 tbsp (13 g) granulated sugar

1 tbsp (15 g) dark brown sugar

Tiny pinch of salt

2 tsp (10 ml) water

¼ tsp ground cinnamon

1 tsp (3 g) cornstarch

Crumble

2 tbsp (20 ml) neutral oil or vegan butter

3 tbsp (23 g) all-purpose flour

3 tbsp (15 g) rolled oats

1½ tbsp (23 g) dark brown sugar

⅛ tsp ground cinnamon

Tiny pinch of salt

To serve: vanilla nice cream (i.e., vegan ice cream)

To begin the filling, peel, core and dice the apple into ⅜-inch (1-cm) cubes. Put them in a bowl and sprinkle with the granulated and brown sugar, salt and water. Mix well and set aside to macerate.

To prepare the crumble, put the oil in a small pan; if you're using butter, melt it over low heat. Sprinkle with the remaining crumble ingredients and stir until crumbly. Toast, stirring often, over medium-low heat for about 5 minutes, or until golden brown. Transfer to a plate to cool.

Back to the filling: Sprinkle the cinnamon and cornstarch over the diced apple and mix well. Transfer the apples and all their juice to a microwave-safe ramekin or large mug. The one I use is 2⅜ inches (6 cm) deep and 4¾ inches (12 cm) wide.

Microwave on high for 2 to 3 minutes, or until the apples are soft and the syrup is bubbling. Each microwave oven is different, so keep an eye on it. You can stop the microwave and give it a stir from time to time (mine takes 3 minutes in my 800-watt microwave).

Remove from the microwave and let cool for a couple of minutes before sprinkling with the crumble topping.

Serve with a scoop of vanilla nice cream.

Snickerdoodle Hummus

If you've seen that dessert hummus in the supermarket and been skeptical about sweet hummus, you don't know what you've been missing. If you've tried them, then you know just how good they are. Luckily, they're so easy and cheaper to make at home!

 Serves 4 to 6

1½ cups (360 g) cooked chickpeas, or 1 (15-oz [425-g]) can, drained and rinsed

2 tbsp (30 g) tahini (optional)

¼ cup (60 ml) full-fat coconut milk

2 tsp (5 g) ground cinnamon

2 tbsp (30 g) dark brown sugar

2 tbsp (15 g) confectioners' sugar

½ tsp vanilla extract

¼ tsp sea salt

Your choice of dippers: sliced apple, pear, strawberries, and vegan pretzels, crackers, cookies, etc.

In a food processor, combine all of the ingredients and blend until smooth. I've made this with and without tahini and the tahini version is creamier, so I recommend it. The non-tahini version is equally delicious but just a bit grainier.

Taste and add more sugar if you want it sweeter, more cinnamon if it's not enough for you.

Serve with fruit or vegan crackers, pretzels or cookies for dipping.

Peanut Butter Pretzel Truffles

Don't bother buying confectioners' sugar for this recipe; you can make it at home by simply grinding white sugar in a blender, spice or coffee grinder. These no-bake truffles are deliciously creamy, sweet and salty bite-size balls of joy. If you love chocolate and you love peanut butter, you'll love these truffles!

 Makes about 16 truffles

½ cup (130 g) peanut butter

¼ cup (30 g) confectioners' sugar

½ cup (50 g) crushed vegan pretzels (see Tip), plus 2 tsp (4 g) for garnish (optional)

7 oz (200 g) vegan dark or baking chocolate

In a medium bowl, mix together the peanut butter and confectioners' sugar. Stir in the crushed pretzels.

Take a heaping 1½-tablespoon (23-ml) measure of this mixture and use your hands to gently roll it into a ball. Place the balls on a parchment paper–lined pan and place it in the freezer for 15 minutes to set.

When 15 minutes are just about up, melt the chocolate. You can do this in a small, microwave-safe bowl in the microwave in 30-second bursts, stirring in between, or in a double boiler on the stovetop.

Use a fork to dip and roll each ball into the chocolate and allow the excess to drip off. Place them back onto the parchment-lined pan and sprinkle with some additional crushed pretzel, if desired.

Chill in the refrigerator to allow the chocolate to set until you're ready to eat, or the freezer if you want them sooner (I know you can't resist).

> **Tip:** You can crush pretzels easily by putting them in a paper or plastic bag and crushing them with a rolling pin or under a mug.

Lemon Lover's Cookies

These vegan cookies are soft and full of sweet lemony flavor, thanks to the fresh lemon juice and zest. An optional and easy lemon glaze on top makes them look extra special.

 Makes 12 to 15 cookies

Cookies

½ cup (120 ml) neutral oil
½ cup (100 g) granulated sugar
2 tsp (10 ml) vanilla extract
¼ cup (60 ml) fresh lemon juice
2 tsp (4 g) fresh lemon zest
2 cups (250 g) all-purpose flour
½ tsp baking powder
¼ tsp salt

Optional Lemon Glaze

2 to 3 tbsp (30 to 45 ml) fresh lemon juice
1 cup (120 g) confectioners' sugar
1 tsp fresh lemon zest

Preheat the oven to 350°F (175°C).

In a bowl, combine the oil, granulated sugar, vanilla and lemon juice and zest. Stir briskly for a minute to dissolve the sugar.

Add the flour, baking powder and salt and stir until combined into a soft dough.

With your hands, roll small portions of the dough into balls. I usually get 12 to 15 cookies from this recipe. Place the balls 2 inches (5 cm) apart on a baking pan and gently flatten them with the palm of your hand.

Bake for 13 to 15 minutes, or until the tops look set and the bottoms are lightly golden, then remove from the oven and let cool on the pan for 2 minutes before using a spatula to transfer them to a wire rack.

Meanwhile, prepare the lemon glaze, if using. In a small bowl, stir together all the glaze ingredients, starting with 1 tablespoon (15 ml) of lemon juice and add more little by little until you have a thick but pourable glaze.

Once the cookies have cooled on the rack for about 10 minutes, drizzle or brush with the glaze or dip the cookies directly into it. Return the cookies to the rack to allow the glaze to set.

Cinnamon Baked Pears

This simple dessert is great for serving to guests, as it looks and tastes more complicated than it is.
You can also do the same with peaches, so feel free to choose whichever fruit is in season and cheaper.

 Serves 4

2 large pears, ripe yet firm (I used Conference)

2 tbsp (15 g) all-purpose flour

2 tbsp (10 g) rolled oats

2 tbsp (30 g) light or dark brown sugar

⅛ tsp salt

1 tbsp (20 ml) plus ½ tsp vegan butter, melted, divided

¼ tsp ground cinnamon

4 scoops vanilla nice cream (i.e., vegan ice cream), for serving

Preheat the oven to 400°F (200°C).

Slice the pears in half lengthwise and use a spoon to scoop out the core. If they don't sit evenly cut side up, cut a small slice off the rounded side.

In a small bowl, combine the flour, oats, brown sugar, salt and 1 tablespoon (15 ml) of the melted vegan butter until crumbly.

Brush the remaining ½ teaspoon of butter over the cut side of the pears and sprinkle with the cinnamon.

Spoon the crumble into the pears and place them, crumble up, in a baking dish. Bake for 10 to 15 minutes, or until the pears are tender and easily pierced with a fork and the crumble is golden.

Let them cool for a few minutes before topping with a scoop of nice cream and serving.

Effortless Chocolate-Covered Stuffed Dates

It's fun to make these all with different fillings so that they're like a box of vegan chocolates. My personal favorite is with a peanut and peanut butter—it almost tastes like a Snickers bar!

 Makes 15 stuffed dates

15 regular dates (see Note)

Your choice of fillings: about ¼ tsp per date of any kind of nut or seed butter (almond, cashew, peanut, tahini, sun butter), 1 or 2 nuts per date (pecans, hazelnuts, peanuts, almonds, walnuts, etc.)

4 oz (113 g) vegan dark chocolate or baking chocolate

Your choice of toppings: chopped nuts, shredded coconut, sesame seeds, crushed vegan pretzels, flaky salt, orange zest

Carefully slice down the center of the dates and remove the pits. Stuff with your choice of filling. You can make them all the same or do a variety of different ones. You can also mix and match with a bit of nut butter and a nut together. Place the stuffed dates on a parchment-lined pan and pop them into the freezer while you prepare the chocolate. If your nut butter is runny, freezing will help make the dipping easier.

Break or chop the chocolate into small pieces and put them in a small, microwave-safe bowl. Microwave in 30-second increments, stirring each time, until melted. You can also do this in a double boiler in the stovetop.

Using a fork, dip each date into the melted chocolate and let the excess run off. Again, here you can be creative: You may want to dip just half the date, the whole thing or even just drizzle a bit of the chocolate over the date. Place them back on the parchment-lined pan.

While the chocolate is still wet, sprinkle with your choice of topping.

Put them back in the freezer or fridge until the chocolate is set.

> Note: By regular dates, I mean not Medjool dates, although you can use Medjool if you want to. Since they're larger, you may not get 15 dates fully dipped in chocolate.

Fresh Peach Turnovers

Since I'm not a lover of sweet breakfasts, I prefer these easy peach turnovers for dessert or an afternoon snack, though they could just as easily double as a breakfast food! Many brands of puff pastry are vegan; just be sure to read the ingredients before buying.

  Serves 6

2 cups (275 g) finely diced peaches

1 to 2 tbsp (15 to 30 g) light or dark brown sugar

½ tsp ground cinnamon

1 tbsp (8 g) all-purpose flour

⅛ tsp salt

1 (17.3-oz [490-g]) package vegan puff pastry (2 sheets), thawed if frozen

½ to 1 tbsp (8 to 15 ml) plant-based milk, plus more for brushing (optional)

½ cup (60 g) confectioners' sugar

Preheat the oven to 400°F (200°C), or according to the directions on the puff pastry. Line a baking sheet with parchment paper.

In a medium bowl, combine the peaches, brown sugar, cinnamon, flour and salt and mix well. If you were lucky to nab superfresh sweet peaches, 1 tablespoon (15 g) of brown sugar should be enough. If you weren't that lucky and they're a bit sour, add 2 tablespoons (30 g), or to taste.

With a sharp knife or pizza cutter, cut each sheet of puff pastry into 6 rectangles and gently transfer half of them to the prepared baking sheet.

Give the peaches a stir and spoon them over the bottom of the tarts, leaving a bit of a border. Place a second rectangle of puff pastry over the first and gently seal the edges with a fork. Gently poke a few holes in the top with a sharp knife to allow steam to vent. Brush each pastry with water or milk.

Bake for 15 to 20 minutes, or until puffy and golden.

In the meantime, combine the confectioners' sugar with enough of the milk to make a thick icing.

Once out of the oven, let the turnovers cool for a few minutes before drizzling with the icing and devouring.

Note: They might not brown as much as puff pastry brushed with an egg wash; I find that different brands of puff pastry brown differently. Some brown well with plant-based milk and others do not.

Chocolaty Peanut Butter–Banana Quesadillas

This recipe is really stupid-easy and dirt cheap. I don't know why I didn't think of it sooner. Once you realize that dessert quesadillas can be a thing, you can let your imagination run wild with all the options for filling them.

 Serves 1

1 tbsp (16 g) smooth or chunky peanut butter, other nut butter, sun butter, or speculoos cookie butter

1 (8"[20-cm]) tortilla

½ medium banana, sliced

1 tbsp (11 g) vegan chocolate chips

Sprinkling of ground cinnamon

Chopped nuts (optional)

1 tsp vegan butter, coconut or other neutral oil or nonstick cooking spray

Optional toppings: a sprinkling of confectioners' sugar, additional melted vegan chocolate drizzled over the top, vegan ice cream, vegan whipped cream

Spread the peanut butter over half of the tortilla. Top with the sliced banana and sprinkle with the chocolate chips and a pinch of cinnamon; add chopped nuts as well, if using. Fold the tortilla in half.

In a skillet, melt the vegan butter over medium heat or lightly spray it with nonstick cooking spray. Cook the tortilla until golden brown, 2 to 3 minutes, then flip and cook until golden brown on the other side and the chocolate chips are melted.

Transfer to a plate and cut into 3 pieces. Serve plain or with the toppings of your choice.

Bananas Foster

Apparently, you can make bananas foster without the alcohol, but why would you? If you're not a rum drinker but want to make a tasty dessert, pick up one of those 50 ml mini bottles. Although it's much better value to get a full-size bottle. I guess you'll have to become a rum drinker.

 Serves 2 or 3

2 ripe bananas
2 tbsp (28 g) vegan butter
2 tbsp (30 g) dark brown sugar
Pinch of ground cinnamon (optional)
Pinch of chopped nuts (optional)
2 tbsp (30 ml) dark rum
Vegan vanilla ice cream
Optional garnish: cherries

Safety first: Choose a large, wide skillet with sloped sides and a long handle for flambéing. Have a tight-fitting lid and a couple of dish towels beside the stove, just in case.

Peel and slice the bananas in half lengthwise and in half widthwise.

In the skillet, heat the butter over medium heat. Add the sugar and a pinch of cinnamon and nuts, if using, and stir until the butter has melted and combined with the additional ingredients. Add the bananas and heat until beginning to brown on one side, about 2 minutes. Gently flip and give them a couple more minutes on the other side. The bananas should be soft and lightly browned.

Turn off the heat. Add the rum, then stand back and ignite the rum with a long-neck lighter or long match. Turn the heat back on and simmer until the flames die, just a few seconds, and the sauce is thickened to your liking.

Add a scoop of nice cream into each serving bowl, top with the bananas and their sauce and garnish with cherries, if desired.

Acknowledgments

First and foremost, I'd like to thank Thai red curry for tasting so good.

Much thanks to Marissa Giambelluca, Will Kiester and the entire team at Page Street Publishing for entrusting some rando from the Internet to deliver an entire book of recipes. I appreciate being given the opportunity to share my passion for vegan food with the world.

Most of all, thank you, Mom, for cooking us homemade meals every single night. I would never have developed an interest in cooking if you'd served us crap every night; just saying.

Thanks, Dad, for your spaghetti and stir-fries and being just generally "cool" in terms of dads.

Thank you, Raúl, for taste-testing every single recipe in this book and even the gross ones that didn't make it into the book. Thanks for your honest feedback of "It's okaaay . . . but I think you can do better."

Thanks to Dora la Exploradora, for being the snuggliest snuggle muffin ever and coming to give me lots of snuggles when I was sitting staring at my computer trying to think of what to write next (like right now).

About the Author

Melissa Copeland is the founder, recipe developer and photographer behind the food blogs The Stingy Vegan and Cilantro & Citronella.

After completing a degree in anthropology, Melissa left her native Canada to learn things about the world that cannot be learned from books. After 15 years abroad, Melissa draws on her knowledge of diverse dishes, spices and cooking techniques when creating vegan recipes for her blogs.

Melissa currently lives in Barcelona, Spain, with her husband and recipe-tester extraordinaire, Raúl, and their fur babies.

Index